Keto Diet Cookbook
for Beginners 2018

The Complete Guide of Ketogenic Diet to Lose
Weight and Overall Health, Have Easy Tasty Low
Carb High Fat Recipes

By Dr. Dave James

Table of Contents

Introduction

Experts have long recognized the fact that lifestyle affects not only one's emotional contentment but also one's overall health. In fact, according to a study (https://www.ncbi.nlm.nih.gov/pubmed/15468523/)by the World Health Organization (WHO), up to 60 percent of health and quality of life are related to lifestyle factors.

Researchers from Iran (https://www.ncbi.nlm.nih.gov/pmc/articles/PMC4703222/) confirmed that diet is the "greatest factor in lifestyle" that directly affects the health. An unhealthy diet can result in obesity, a common problem in modern urban societies.

The Centers for Disease Control and Prevention (CDC) (https://www.cdc.gov/obesity/data/adult.html)eported that up to 36 percent of adults in the United States are obese, and are therefore at risk of numerous obesity-related ailments such as stroke, heart disease, type 2 diabetes, and certain forms of cancer.
It's for this reason that experts have worked continually in researching and formulating healthy diets, and promoting these to the public.

One of the healthy diet programs that have emerged in the recent years is the ketogenic diet. Originally designed for patients with epilepsy, the ketogenic diet has also been discovered to be an effective weight loss tool, helping people shed unwanted pounds and at the same time, promoting overall health.

In this book, we shall discuss everything that you need to know about this diet program should you want to get started with it. It covers the guidelines and basic components, the process of getting into the process of ketosis, the benefits of the keto diet, and many more.

That's not all. Since it can be quite challenging getting started on any diet program, we have provided recipes that are not only simple and easy to cook, but are also conveniently prepared using the Instant Pot or slow cooker.

Good luck on your journey to a healthier you!

Chapter 1 – Essential Basics You Need to Know About Keto Diet

What's the Keto Diet?

The ketogenic diet comes in various names—low carb diet, low carb high fat diet, keto diet, and so on.

Basically, it is based on the principle of encouraging the body to produce ketones as energy source.

Here's how it works:

When people eat foods that are rich in carbohydrates, the body produces **glucose** and **insulin**.

Glucose can easily be converted into energy, which is why the body prefers it as energy source.

Insulin, meanwhile, is produced so that the body can use it to process the glucose.

If the body uses glucose as energy source, fats take a backseat. They are not utilized, and are instead stored in the tissues. The more fats stored, the more a person gains weight.

If you reduce the intake of carbohydrates, the body goes through a process of **ketosis**.

During this process, the body breaks down the fats from the food eaten and from those that are stored in the tissues. As a result, the body produces ketones, and this is what it uses for energy.

Is Keto Diet Suitable for Me?

The ketogenic is ideal for most people who want to lose weight, prevent ailments, and promote overall health.

As mentioned earlier, it is designed for people who suffer from epilepsy. Its efficacy as treatment aid has been proven in scientific research (https://www.ncbi.nlm.nih.gov/pmc/articles/PMC2902940/).

Athletes who want to power up fat metabolism are also encouraged to adopt this diet program.

It's important to know however that this diet is not for everyone.

It is not recommended for people who have been diagnosed with any kidney disease, liver disease or pancreatic disease. Although this has been used by diabetic patients, anyone who has any blood sugar issues should first consult a doctor before using this diet.

Moreover, pregnant and nursing women are not advised to follow the keto diet.

What is The Ketosis?

Ketosis is a metabolic process that a body undergoes when it does not receive enough carbohydrates to use for energy. In order to keep working, the body looks for alternative source of energy so it turns to the fat stored in your tissues or those obtained from foods that you consume.

As mentioned earlier, this process produces organic compounds called **ketones**, which the body converts into energy. This is the main principle by which the ketogenic diet works—by prompting the body to go into ketosis through a low carb diet, it burns fat instead of carbs, helping you lose weight along the way.

Actionable Ways to Identify if You Are in Ketosis or Not

There are two ways to determine if you have reached the state of ketosis:
- Measure the ketones inside your body
- Look for signs and symptoms of ketosis

3 Ways to Measure Ketones

To measure ketone level, you can use the following tools:
- **Urine sticks** – A urine stick is a cheap device that you can use to measure the number of ketones in your body. However, the accuracy rate is quite low.
- **Breath ketone meter** – This is used to measure the ketones in your breath. It is more expensive than the urine stick but more accurate.
- **Blood ketone meter** – This is the most expensive and most accurate tool that you can use to measure ketone level in the body.

5 Signs and Symptoms of Ketosis

Watch out for these signs and symptoms so you will know if you have reached the state of ketosis or not.
- **More frequent urination** – The keto diet is a natural diuretic.
- **Dry mouth** – This is usually accompanied by increased thirst.
- **Bad breath** – Bad breath is caused by the acetone by product from the ketones that are partially excreted through the breath.
- **Increased energy levels** – Once your body has adjusted to the diet, you will feel more energetic.

- **Reduced hunger** – The keto diet has also been proven to reduce hunger pangs and suppress cravings especially for sweets.

How to Get into Ketosis Step-by-Step?

Reaching the state of ketosis is actually very simple. The steps are outlined below:
- **Reduce intake of carbohydrates** – To get optimal results, one needs to reduce intake not only of net carbs but also of total carbs. It's ideal to limit intake to 20 grams net carbs and 35 grams total carbs per day.
- **Limit protein consumption** – Most people focus only on the carb intake, not realizing that protein should also be reduced. It's important to keep in mind that excessive protein can hamper the process of ketosis. It's best to keep your protein intake to 0.6 grams and 0.8 grams per pound of lean body mass. Use a keto calculator (https://www.ruled.me/keto-calculator) to help you determine your ideal protein intake.
- **Don't reduce fat intake** – Fat will be the main source of energy for your body while you're on the ketogenic diet so there's no need to limit intake. However, it'd be a good idea to rely more on healthy fats (http://www.health.com/health/gallery/0,,20477647,00.html).
- **Keep yourself hydrated** – As mentioned earlier, dry mouth and increased thirst are some of the symptoms of ketosis. This is why, you need to drink eight to 10 glasses of water or more a day. This will help regulate the essential bodily processes as well as reduce hunger pangs.
- **Limit snacking** – Snacking slows down weight loss and spikes up the insulin levels.
- **Get regular exercise** – It's not wise to take on any weight loss diet without exercise. Aim for at least 30 minutes of moderate aerobic exercise a day.

Basically, you need to maintain this percentage of macronutrients:
- **Fats** – 60 to 80 percent of daily calories
- **Protein** – 20 to 25 percent of daily calories
- **Carbohydrates** – 5 to 10 percent of daily calories

Know about The Ketones

Also called **ketone bodies**, ketones refer to the by-products of the body after it metabolizes fat to be used for energy.

There are three types of ketones:
- Acetoacetate (AcAc)
- Beta-hydroxybutyric acid (BHB)
- Acetone

Acetoacetate and beta-hydroxybutyrate transport energy from the liver to other parts of the body. Meanwhile, acetone is a by-product that is excreted through urine or breath.

What is The Reasonable Quantity of Carb Intake?

It's important to know that people have different carb limits. Generally, it is advised to stay below 35 grams of total carbs and 25 grams of net carbs.

You can determine net carbs by subtracting fiber grams from the total carbs. Staying within this limit helps you achieve ketosis and maintain this metabolic state. But as said earlier, it's also important not to consume excessive amounts of protein.

Does Keto Diet and Atkins Diet Same?

The Atkins Diet became popular in the early 2000s as a diet program promoting weight loss and better health. It was introduced by Dr. Robert Coleman Atkins, after discovering in 1963 that carbohydrate reduction resulted in weight loss.

This diet has undergone many changes but currently, there are two main types:

- **Atkins 20** – This is designed for people who intend to lose more than 40 pounds.
- **Atkins 40** – This is a less-restrictive type for those who intend to lose less than 40 pounds.

Compared to the Atkins Diet, the ketogenic diet appears to have more benefits.

For one, keto is more a lifestyle while Atkins is a short-term weight loss program. With the latter, there's less chance of maintaining long-term results.

With the Atkins Diet, carbs are re-introduced into the diet after the initial phase. In the phases following the initial stage, people are prompted to consume up to 100 grams of carbs a day.

This leads to the person gaining back the weight that he initially lost. This scenario does not happen with ketogenic dieters as long as they continue following the program.

During the initial phase, the two diet programs appear to be similar. But most people who have tried both diet programs can attest that keto is what you should go for if you want long-lasting results.

Any Difference Between Low Carb Diet and Keto Diet?

Keto is often called the low carb diet, but it's important to realize that a low carb diet is actually different.

While both types of diet programs limit carb intake, take note that the keto diet also regulates protein consumption. Lowering intake of carbohydrates is futile if you keep consuming too much protein.

Excessive protein is known to hamper the process of ketosis. It is for this reason that many people find the keto diet more effective than any other low carb diet program.

Chapter 2: Some Unbelievable Benefits of Keto Diet

One of the reasons the keto diet has become popular all over the world is not only because it is effective as a weight loss program, but also because it has many other benefits for the health. Below, you will understand how the keto diet helps you shed unwanted pounds, and at the same time, keep you in top shape.

1. It Balances Your Blood Sugar Levels

A high level of blood sugar is not good for you. It causes unpleasant side effects such as fatigue, headache, difficulty in concentrating, and blurry vision, among others.

Not only that, it also shoots up the risk of type 2 diabetes. The CDC (https://www.cdc.gov/media/releases/2014/p0610-diabetes-report.html) reports that in the United States alone, there are now over 29 million people who suffer from this condition.

What's the cause? Experts agree that type 2 diabetes can be a result of unhealthy diet and lifestyle. Processed food products such as cakes, candies and pastries, as well as naturally starchy foods like potatoes and rice can increase blood sugar levels.

You'll know that you have high blood sugar levels if you experience increased thirst, headaches, frequent urination, weakness, and unexplained weight loss. Blood sugar that is more than 180 mg/dL is considered high.

If this happens frequently, it can lead to the following:

- Blood floor reduction
- Increased risk of stroke, heart attack and type 2 diabetes
- Nerve damage
- Blindness
- Kidney failure

The good news is you can prevent type 2 diabetes along with other chronic ailments, and control blood sugar levels with the help of the ketogenic diet.

The keto diet has been found to be more effective than low-calorie diets in reducing the risk of these ailments.

In a study (https://www.ncbi.nlm.nih.gov/pmc/articles/PMC1325029/) published in the *Nutrition & Metabolism Journal*, it was found that the keto diet can successfully improve high blood sugar levels, and even reduce the intake of medications among patients diagnosed with type 2 diabetes.

A total of 28 overweight patients with diabetes underwent a 16-week study in which they were asked to undergo a diet that reduced daily carb intake to less than 20 grams.

Results showed that the body mass index (BMI) for most of the participants reduced significantly. The blood sugar level also decreased, and a few of the patients were able to discontinue or reduce the use of medications.

Despite these findings, it is important to remember that one should consult a doctor first before taking on the keto diet as treatment aid for diabetes.

2. It Manages Your Blood Pressure Levels

Like blood sugar levels, blood pressure levels should also be controlled.

Blood pressure refers to the amount of pressure exerts by the blood on the blood vessel walls. This is determined through two numbers:

- **Systolic pressure** – This is the top number which is the amount of the pressure in the arteries during heart contraction.
- **Diastolic pressure** – This indicates the pressure in the arteries during the beating of the heart.

Both numbers are express in millimetres of mercury (mm Hg).

The standard or healthy blood pressure level is 120/80 mm Hg. If a person has 121/81 mm Hg to 139/90 mm Hg blood pressure level, he/she will typically be diagnosed with pre-hypertension.

If not given immediate attention, this can lead to hypertension. Hypertension is a condition characterized by blood pressure levels above 140/90 mm Hg. This can lead to several complications such as kidney failure, stroke, heart attack, heart failure, and even death.

According to the Blood Pressure UK (http://www.bloodpressureuk.org/mediacentre/FAQs), one in three adults has high blood pressure. This is quite alarming, and should be given sufficient attention.

Managing blood pressure levels is possible with the right diet and regular exercise. It's also important to regularly undergo blood pressure screening.

Research has shown that the keto diet can help maintain proper levels of blood pressure.

A study (https://www.ncbi.nlm.nih.gov/pmc/articles/PMC4666896/) conducted by a team of scientists from Italy reported that the keto diet can improve various cardiovascular risk factors including high blood pressure. Researchers recommend further randomized trials to confirm their findings.

For most people, this can be quite surprising since high fat diets have always been associated with high blood pressure.

A 2015 study (http://europepmc.org/abstract/med/26602244)counters this with evidence showing that a low fat, high carb diet can actually increase blood pressure levels.

If you have been diagnosed with prehypertension or hypertension, check with your doctor first before undergoing the keto diet.

3. It Maintains Proper Cholesterol Levels

One of the most popular misconceptions about the keto diet is that because it's high in fat, it automatically shoots up cholesterol levels.

But research has proven otherwise. Recent studies show that a low carb diet can in fact lower cholesterol levels and reduce the risk of heart disease.

Before we get to that, it's important to first understand the functions of cholesterol and fat in the body.

Also called lipids, fats are molecules known to repel water. It is present in the bloodstream in two forms:

- **Triglycerides** – This refers to a fatty acid that stores energy, and can be metabolized to be used as fuel. An increase in the triglycerides can lead to the onset of heart disease and diabetes.
- **Cholesterol** – This refers to the waxy substance that has many roles in the body such as producing hormones, helping absorb vitamins, strengthens the cell membranes and so on. This substance is produced by the body through the liver. It can also be derived from foods such as red meat, dairy and poultry.

Cholesterol can be further broken down into five forms:

- Chylomicrons
- Very-low-density lipoproteins (VLDL)
- Intermediate-density lipoproteins (IDL)
- Low-density lipoproteins (LDL)
- High-density lipoproteins (HDL)

In this section, we are going to focus more on the HDL and LDL cholesterol.

HDL cholesterol is often called the "good cholesterol". Its primary role is to transport cholesterol throughout the body, and to collect those that not utilized by the cells so that it can either be recycled or removed in the liver.

It has been dubbed as the good cholesterol because it prevents cholesterol from building up and clogging the arteries. Having high HDL levels is actually good for the health.

The ideal range for HDL is 40 to 60 mg/dl for men, and 50 to 60 mg/dl for women.

LDL cholesterol, on the other hand, is referred to as the "bad cholesterol". But it's more complicated than most people realize. Yes, the LDL also helps in the transportation of the cholesterol in the body. The problem is, it is more susceptible to oxidation by harmful substances called **free radicals**. Aside from that, the LDL can also attach to the arterial walls and hamper proper functioning of the heart. This is why an increase in LDL cholesterol levels can be quite alarming as this means that you will be at an increased risk of heart disease.

It's ideal to maintain LDL levels at below 100 mg/dL. Some people can have LDL levels of up to 129 mg/dL without experiencing any problem. However, those who have health issues or are at risk of heart disease should make an effort to maintain proper LDL cholesterol level.

In 2004, researchers from Kuwait
(https://www.ncbi.nlm.nih.gov/pmc/articles/PMC2716748/)evaluated the effects of a 24-week
ketogenic diet among obese patients.

A total of 83 obese patients with BMI greater than 35 kg/m2 and who suffer from high cholesterol
levels participated in this study. Aside from the body weight, the participants' HDL, LDL and
triglyceride levels were also measured.

After the study, it was found that the BMI of the participants decreased significantly. It was also
noted in the findings that the HDL cholesterol levels increased while the LDL cholesterol and
triglyceride levels were reduced. Researchers confirmed that the keto diet has positive effects on
cholesterol levels.

4. It Helps in Weight Loss

For most people, losing weight is all about looking better, and feeling more confident. But what
many take for granted is how maintaining the right weight can help avert many types of illnesses.
Obesity has been linked to numerous conditions including heart disease, stroke, diabetes, certain
types of cancer, gallbladder disease, osteoarthritis, gout, and breathing problems.

Alarmingly, obesity has become a major problem in many parts of the world. The WHO
(http://www.who.int/news-room/fact-sheets/detail/obesity-and-overweight)reports that obesity
has increased in trifold since 1975, and that over 1.9 billion people are overweight.

Adopting a healthy diet is a step towards healthy weight loss. Many studies have provided evidence
that the keto diet is effective in helping people lose weight.

Although primarily designed as treatment for epilepsy, the keto diet's claim to fame in the modern
society is its ability to shed unwanted pounds. More and more people are using this diet program as a
weight loss tool, and have found success in doing so.

A meta-analysis (https://www.ncbi.nlm.nih.gov/pubmed/23651522/)of several randomized
controlled trials showed that the keto diet is highly effective in reducing weight and BMI.
Researchers noted that those who use the low carbohydrate diet lost significantly more weight than
those who adopted the low-fat diet, indicating that very low carb keto diet can be an "alternative
tool against obesity".

5. It Regulates Your Appetite

A benefit related to weight loss is the keto diet's ability to regulate the appetite.

As we all know, cravings are some of the major hindrances in a dieter's weight loss journey. It
becomes a lot more difficult to lose weight if you are constantly craving for unhealthy snacks and
treats.

According to Mind Body Green (https://www.mindbodygreen.com/articles/a-doctor-on-why-ketosis-helps-you-lose-weight), ketosis is a **"great appetite suppressant"**. Anyone following a standard western diet that's high in carbohydrates is prone to experience "blood sugar swings" that cause hunger pangs. Sometimes, one will start to crave for food only one to two hours after finishing meal.

But once you're in the process of ketosis, the body will start to burn fat for energy, which in turn stabilizes the blood sugar levels. Fat will be metabolized in the liver. As a result, hunger pangs will be reduced significantly.

Moreover, ketosis also affects the levels of **ghrelin**, which is the hunger hormone that makes you want to eat more. When you're in a keto diet, the ghrelin hormone drops, and you will no longer experience frequent cravings.

This is not a baseless claim. In fact, it was noted in a 2014 study (https://www.ncbi.nlm.nih.gov/pmc/articles/PMC3945587/)published in the *International Journal of Environmental Research and Public Health* that the keto diet reduces appetite through the satiety effect of protein intake and effect on hunger hormones. It is also believed that the ketone bodies also have "appetite suppressant action".

6. It Helps You Get Rid of Visceral Fat

More popularly known as belly fat, **visceral fat** is not only unsightly but also dangerous. This type of deep gel-like fat that covers major organs such as the kidneys, liver and pancreas can increase the risk of the following diseases:

- Cancer
- Heart disease
- Stroke
- Diabetes
- Dementia
- Depression
- Arthritis
- Sexual dysfunction

Aside from increasing the risk of these conditions, the excess fat can also disrupt the normal functioning of the hormones, and at the same time, promote the production of pro-inflammatory chemicals known as **cytokines**.

Most people who have belly fat will probably agree that it can be very difficult to get rid of.

The good news is, you can finally say goodbye to stubborn belly fat with the help of the keto diet.

But before we get to that, let's first understand why it's challenging to remove belly fat.

To understand what makes belly fat so difficult to burn, let's dive into the biology.

Burning fat has two stages:

- **Lipolysis** – This refers to the process in which the fat cells release the molecules of stored fat into the bloodstream.
- **Oxidation** – In the process of oxidation, cells burn the stored fat.

The process of lipolysis is stimulated by **catecholamines**, which may be impeded by alpha receptors and triggered by beta receptors.

Visceral fat contains fat cells that have more alpha receptors, which explains why it is more difficult than other types of fat to burn.

When one undergoes a ketogenic diet, the body has no choice but to burn fat for energy, even the stubborn ones such as the fat in the belly area. It's for this reason that those who struggle with visceral fat have found great success in the keto diet.

7. Helping with Metabolic Syndrome

Metabolic syndrome is not just one condition. It is actually a cluster of several conditions including high blood pressure, high blood sugar, high cholesterol and excess visceral fat, all occurring at the same time, shooting up the risk for diabetes, stroke and heart disease.

The exact cause is unknown. However, experts agree that it is triggered by obesity and sedentary lifestyle. It can also be associated with insulin resistance.

If you are at risk of metabolic syndrome or have been diagnosed with this condition, the keto diet can certainly help.

In a 2017 study (https://static1.squarespace.com/static/59ae01e849fc2b19c93fbb46/t/5a028ceeec212d79d86caf4e/1510 116592216/Diabetes+%26+Metabolic+Syndrome-+Clinical+Research+%26+Reviews.pdf)conducted by American researchers, it was reported that the keto diet may reverse the process that triggers that onset of metabolic syndrome.

A group of 30 patients diagnosed with metabolic syndrome participated in this experiment. The first group followed a keto diet with no exercise. The second group used the standard American diet with no exercise. The third group was required to undergo the standard American diet with 30 minutes of daily exercise for five days.

After 10 weeks, findings revealed that the first group had significant reduction in BMI, body fat percentage and weight. They also had lower levels of A1C (https://medlineplus.gov/a1c.html)(a measure of average blood glucose).

It was concluded that the keto diet was effective than the standard American diet even when combined with exercise in reducing the risk of metabolic syndrome.

8. Helping with Cognitive Disorders

Cognitive disorders remain a major issue in many countries around the world. The WHO (http://www.who.int/bulletin/volumes/91/10/13-118422/en/)estimates that there are currently about 35 million people who suffer from dementia worldwide. The rate is expected to double in 20 years.

Also called neurocognitive disorders, cognitive disorders refer to a classification of mental health problems that disrupt cognitive skills and abilities including memory, learning, problem solving and perception, among others.

Some of the most common cognitive disorders are dementia, autism and Down syndrome. Dyslexia and attention deficit disorder (ADD) are also considered as cognitive conditions but are less severe.

Although the keto diet cannot treat or reverse Down Syndrome and other cognitive conditions, it has been found to be effective in enhancing memory among elderly people with mild cognitive impairment.

A team of American researchers (https://www.ncbi.nlm.nih.gov/pmc/articles/PMC3116949/)divided a group of 23 elderly adults with mild cognitive impairment into two groups. The first group followed a high carbohydrate diet while the second group was made to take a low carbohydrate diet. After six weeks, the researchers noted significant improvement in memory performance among those who followed the low carbohydrate diet.

This positive effect could be attributed to the ability of ketosis to reduce inflammation as well as improve energy metabolism, both of which can lead to better cognitive function.

9. It Improvs Your Mental Health

Not surprisingly, the keto diet appears to have a positive effect not only on cognition but on general mental health.

According to its proponents, the keto diet has numerous benefits for the brain, including boosting the mood, enhancing brain function, neutralizing free radical damage, and promoting the production of "feel good" neurotransmitters.

While in ketosis, the brain produces more of the neurotransmitter called **GABA**. Studies have shown that many anxiety related disorders stem from reduced GABA activity in the brain. Experts also agree that increased GABA levels can help reduce stress and anxiety and at the same time, improve mental focus.

Not only that, keto dieters are also found to be at less risk of depression. The ketogenic diet's antidepressive effects were confirmed in a 2004 study (https://www.ncbi.nlm.nih.gov/pubmed/15601609)featured in the *Biological Psychiatry Journal*.

It is also interesting to note that the ketones produced during ketosis can power up the brain more effectively than glucose, as reported in a 2005 study (http://onlinelibrary.wiley.com/doi/10.1002/bmb.2005.49403304246/full).

Chapter 3: Symptoms with Solutions During Keto Diet

While it's true that the keto diet has many scientifically proven benefits, it's not without side effects and risks. If you are going to follow this diet, it's very important to know all about these so you can be prepared, and you will know what exactly you have to do.

Ketogenic Flu

One of the most common complaints among keto dieters is the **keto flu.**

Also called the "carb flu", the keto flu refers to the withdrawal process that the body undergoes after transitioning from a high carb to a low carb diet. It signals that the body is adjusting from using sugar as energy to burning fat for fuel.

According to some keto dieters, this condition is similar to withdrawal from addictive substances, which is not a surprise since sugar has been dubbed as the "cocaine of the food world".

The following are some of the common symptoms of the keto flu:

- Cravings
- Dizziness and lightheadedness
- Brain fog
- Inability to focus
- Nausea
- Muscle camping
- Confusion
- Irritability
- Stomach ache
- Insomnia

For most people, these symptoms last for about a week and can go away without any intervention. But if the keto flu takes longer than two to three weeks, it can be a sign that the body is not adjusting well.

To manage your keto flu symptoms, here are some tips to follow:

- **Replenish your supply of electrolytes** – Drink electrolyte beverages or take electrolyte supplements. Make sure that your electrolyte beverage or supplement does not contain sugar and artificial sweeteners. You can also make your own by mixing one cup water, one teaspoon sea salt and one teaspoon lemon juice.
- **Keep yourself hydrated** – Aside from electrolytes, you also need to make sure that you have enough fluids in your body. If not, you will feel tired, sluggish and will probably suffer from episodes of headaches. Drink eight to 10 glasses of water each day, or even more if you're active.
- **Use bone broth as remedy** – Bone broth is a good remedy for keto flu. Not only does it provide the electrolytes you need (potassium and sodium), it also keeps your body hydrated. Of course, homemade bone broth is the preferred for treating the keto flu.
- **Consume more fat** – Yes, you heard it right. Instead of slowing down on fat intake, you can eat more to help the body adjust more quickly. But remember to load up on healthy fats only such as avocado, olive oil, nuts and seeds and so on.

- **Get moving** – Although you're feeling weak and tired, and would probably want to stay in bed the whole day, the best way to relieve the keto flu symptoms is to get moving. There's no need to engage in strenuous exercises. A gentle walk in the park will do. This will relieve muscle cramping and pain, and at the same time, boost the mood and make you feel better.
- **Get good quality sleep** – Some people complain that the keto flu makes it difficult for them to fall or stay asleep. One thing that you can do is to soak in a warm salt bath. This will effectively relax the muscles and soothe your senses. That's not all, it will also boost the electrolyte absorption. Best to use for this purpose is magnesium salts. It's also a good idea to refrain from using gadgets an hour or two before sleeping. The blue light emitted by smart phones and other tech gadgets disrupt the body's circadian rhythm, making it difficult for a person to fall asleep.

Bad Breath

Bad breath is a common side effect not only of the keto diet but also of other low carb diets. This is caused by the ketones that in turn produce acetone that's released through the breath. Experts assure that this is not a hygiene issue. Unfortunately, it cannot be resolved with brushing or flossing. So what can you do instead? Drinking more water helps. It keeps the mouth moist, preventing bacteria from reproducing. It also helps the organs function more effectively, burning fat more easily.

Headaches

During the first week of the keto diet, most people suffer from mild to moderate episodes of headaches.
There are three possible causes:

- Dehydration
- Sugar or carbohydrate withdrawal
- Electrolyte imbalance

Some people experience headaches for only one day, while for others the problem can go on for over a week. To resolve this symptom, it's best to keep yourself hydrated with enough water. It also helps to increase consumption of sodium by drinking bone broth.
Headaches can also be averted with the help of supplements. Some of the recommended supplements include:

- L-carnitine
- Co-Enzyme Q10
- Omega-3 fatty acids

Moreover, a few experts recommend avoiding protein during the first phase of the keto diet, limiting intake to 25 percent of overall calorie intake.

Leg Cramps

Cramps especially in the legs are a typical occurrence among those who are just starting out on the keto diet. Leg cramps usually take place in the morning or in the evening. It indicates deficiency in minerals, particularly in magnesium.
Drinking plenty of fluids and taking magnesium supplements can help.

Temporary Fatigue

It's also normal to experience fatigue during the start of the keto diet. When the body is transitioning from one diet to another, it typically undergoes major processes that would make you feel tired and sluggish.
The best way to fight fatigue is with exercise. Yes, you would probably want to get a lot of rest. And that's good too. However, if you want your energy back, you should get moving. A 30-minute mild to moderate intensity aerobic exercise daily is recommended to combat fatigue.

Difficulty Sleeping

Some people also find it difficult to sleep while on a keto diet. This can be due to the other symptoms such as the keto flu, headaches, or cramping.
As mentioned earlier, soaking in a salt bath can help induce good quality sleep. It's also a must to turn off tech gadgets an hour or two before going to bed.

Constipation

Constipation is most commonly caused by dehydration. The most effective solution? To increase intake of water, that is. It's also a smart move to take in more fiber from non-starchy vegetables as this helps the bowel to move more efficiently. If this doesn't work to relieve your constipation, try taking in a probiotic or using psyllium husk powder.

Chapter 4: Secrets of Producing Inadequate Ketones

Achieving ketosis is the primary step in the journey towards the ketogenic diet success. However, not everyone is able to reach this state as immediately as they expect. For some, it seems like no matter what they do, the diet program does not seem to work.

There are some cases in which the body does not produce enough ketones to reach the state of ketosis.

And there are many possible reasons for this. Enumerated below are the reasons deemed by experts as hindrances to ketosis success.

Secret 1 – Consumption of hidden carbohydrates

As much as possible you've tried to stay away from foods with high carbs namely grains, bread, pasta, and so on. In fact, you've done a great job sticking to the foods that are on the "foods to eat" list.

But even so, you're still not getting the results that you're hoping for. The problem? Hidden carbohydrates.

Be aware that there are certain foods like nuts, dairy and some types of vegetables that are in fact keto-approved that contain more carbs than you think.

It's best to consume dairy and nuts in moderation. And if you're going to prepare dishes that contain cruciferous vegetables such as broccoli, cabbage or cauliflower, limit the amount that you'll include.

Secret 2 – Not eating enough food

Surprisingly, not eating enough food can also have the same effect on your keto diet.

If you're taking in less than the right amount of calories, the body will go into starvation mode and slow down the metabolism to enable you to have energy left to use throughout the day.

This is why, you need to ensure that you're taking in proper number of calories, fat and other nutrients.

Secret 3 – Leptin resistance

Leptin is a hormone that signals the brain that you're full after eating. It is in charge of regulating the number of calories you take in, the amount of fat stored in the body, and how much of these are burned. This hormone is produced by the fat cells inside the body.

If you suffer from **leptin resistance**, which means that even though the body produces enough of this hormone, the brain does not receive its messages, this can have a negative effect on your ketogenic diet.

Leptin resistance can be caused by a number of factors, the most common of which include lack of sleep, unhealthy diet, stress, over eating, and slow metabolism. You need to do something about leptin resistance to be able to get to your goals more quickly.

Secret 4 – Excessive consumption of protein

So you've reduced your carb intake and increased consumption of healthy fats. How come the diet is still not working? It's possible that you are consuming too much protein.

When you're on a ketogenic diet, you only need enough amount of protein to help the muscles recover. Take note that if you consume too much of this nutrient, it will prevent the body from achieving the state of ketosis. This is due to **gluconeogenesis**.

Gluconeogenesis refers to a metabolic process in which protein that you consume is converted into glycogen. What happens is that the body remains dependent on glucose as source of energy. Therefore, it will not use fat as fuel, defeating the primary purpose of ketosis. It's imperative that you consume just the right amount of protein so as not to hamper the process of ketosis from taking place.

Secret 5 - Stress

Stress is a part of most people's daily lives. While it's good to experience stress from time to time as it heightens alertness and helps a person come up with quick actions, chronic stress is bad for the health.

It can also hamper the process of ketosis, preventing weight loss. That's because when one is stressed out, the body releases the hormone cortisol, which is also the one in charge for storing fat in the abdominal area.

If you're on a ketogenic diet but you find yourself constantly stressed out, you need to take a break and make use of stress-reduction techniques to achieve the goals that you want.

Listening to soothing music, taking a warm bath, reading a book or catching up with friends are some of the effective ways to de-stress. You should also try breathing exercises, yoga, meditation and massage therapy, which have worked wonders for people who suffer from chronic stress.

Secret 6 – Eating too much food

Some people make the mistake of thinking that just because the keto diet is a high fat diet, there's no limit to the amount of fat that they can consume.

But you'd have to remember, if you eat a lot of fat, you're going to end up taking in a lot of calories. As you know, fats have twice more calories than proteins or carbs. This makes it imperative for you to be mindful of your fat intake so you know how many calories you are consuming.

It helps to use a keto macro calculator (https://www.perfectketo.com/keto-macro-calculator/) to determine how many calories you need to take in based on your age, body fat, weight, height, physical activity and weight loss goals.

Secret 7 – Too much exercise

It's true what they say that too much of a good thing can be bad. This is also true with exercise. Yes, exercise is essential not only to weight loss but to overall health and fitness. However, if you're over exercising, you will end up eating more than you should to replace the burned calories and to keep your energy levels up.

Not only that, over exercising can also increase the risk of internal inflammation and oxidative stress. Aim for a minimum of 30 minutes of aerobic exercise per day. You can go for as long as one to two hours. But do not spend the whole day jogging or running on the treadmill.

Secret 8 – Lack of sleep

Another factor that can prevent the body from reaching the state of ketosis is lack of sleep. Sleep deprivation has always been known to be a factor that prevents weight loss.

Here's what happens: if you don't get enough sleep, the circadian rhythms are disrupted, affecting the proper functioning of the body's internal organs. As a result, the body will not burn the calories the way it should.

Sleep also plays an important role in the proper balance of hormones. **Ghrelin**, the hormone that signals hunger, increases due to lack of sleep. This means that you will have more cravings if you're not getting enough eyeshut at night.

Secret 9 – Food Sensitivity

Some people have sensitivities to certain types of food without even knowing it.

For example, you might be sensitive to dairy, and this might be causing an imbalance in your digestive tract without you being aware of it. This can lead to inflammation, which in turn contributes to weight gain as well as increases the risk of a number of diseases.

If you suspect that you have any food sensitivity, monitor your reaction to certain foods and determine which ones you should avoid or limit intake of.

Chapter 5: Most Useful Tips for a Successful Keto Diet

Anyone following the ketogenic diet has one goal in mind: success.

Now, the definition of success can be any of the following:
- Lose a specific amount of weight
- Make a change towards a healthier lifestyle
- Look better and feel better
- Reduce the risk of serious ailments

Success can also mean all of the above! Whatever is your definition of success, allow us to help you get there. Here are some tips that will do just that.

1 - Follow the Keto Diet Step by Step

Below, you will find the step by step procedure of the keto diet program. Be sure to follow each step carefully:

Step #1 – Prepare yourself

It's not only your body that should be prepared for a new diet, but also your mind.

First, you need to set your mind that this is not going to be a walk in the park, that throughout your journey, you will be experiencing numerous hardships and challenges, some of which would even make you want to quit at some point.

If you are prepared for such scenario, it will be so much easier for you to overcome difficulties than if you have no idea of what to expect.

Second, you need to equip yourself with enough knowledge about the ketogenic diet. Yes, this book already provides almost everything you need to know. But there's a plethora of information online about this diet program just in case if you have any more questions. Just make sure that you rely only on reliable sources.

It's also important to prepare not only yourself but also your home and the people around you. Talk to your family about this new diet program you are embarking, as you will need their support and encouragement. Look around your home, particularly your kitchen, and take the time to discard unhealthy food items in there that will tempt you to veer away from the keto diet.

Step # 2 – Measure yourself

Before you can get started with the keto diet, you need to first measure yourself. This will determine your starting point and enable you to track your progress effectively.

Here are the stats that you need to know:

- Weight
- Height
- Hips
- Thigh
- Calf
- Wrist
- Forearm

Once you know all these stats, you can use a BMI calculator to find out your BMI and body fat percentage.

Step # 3 – Know the macros

After you've gathered the essential information about your body's current stats, you can go ahead and make use of a keto calculator (https://ketosizeme.com/personal-keto-macro-calculator/)to determine how many carbohydrates, protein and fat you need to consume to be able to reach the goals that you desire. It's not enough to have a rough idea of these numbers. You need specific figures. Write them down so you don't forget.

Generally, experts recommend limiting net carbs to 20 grams and total carbs to 35 grams per day. As for protein, it's good to keep it within 0.6 grams and 0.8 grams per pound lean body mass.

Step # 4 – Plan your meals

The next thing that you have to do is to plan your meals. Write down a weekly menu consisting of dishes that are keto-friendly. In the next chapters of this book, you will find recipes that can help you in your meal planning.

Step # 5 – Monitor your progress

Monitor your progress each week by taking note of the stats that you previously measured in the second step. Keeping a journal will help you track your progress.

2 – Must Be Careful When Eating Out

For most people, eating out is a break from the chore of cooking and food preparation. It's also bonding time with family or friends. Now that you're on a keto diet, you might be thinking that you will no longer be allowed to dine out. This is not true.

As long as you're careful with your choices not only on food but also on restaurants (and dining partners too), you should not have any problem.

Here are some pointers to remember:

- **Do your research before eating out** – Use the internet to find out the menu of the restaurant you're planning to visit. This way, you can already decide which foods to order when you get there.
- **Eat before leaving the house** – You don't have to eat a full meal but this is just to ensure that you don't arrive at the restaurant too hungry. It's a lot more difficult to stick to your diet when you're very hungry.
- **Go for keto-friendly restaurants** – Some restaurants serve keto-friendly dishes. These include: seafood restaurants, restaurants that serve Greek, Middle Eastern and Mediterranean fare, and grill/barbecue restaurants. It's also a good idea to avoid eating at pizza joints, Italian restaurants, Mexican eateries, sandwich shops and fast food joints.
- **Ask questions** – If you're not sure whether the food you want to order is keto friendly or not, ask the server. For example, you can inquire whether the fish or meat is breaded, or if it comes with high carb sauces or toppings.
- **Dine with the right people** – Don't go out with people who will judge your food choices or make negative comments about your diet. Go out with those who are positive and supportive, and whom you will enjoy dining with.

3 - Change Your Pantry with Keto Foods

If your pantry is loaded with foods that are not on the "foods to eat" list, you are going to have a harder time sticking to your diet.
Take a good look at your pantry and also your refrigerator and freezer. Let go of all candies, chocolates, ice cream, cereals, crackers, bread and so on. Give food to charity or local food bank.
If this is not possible because there are other people at home who are not using the same diet as you, then it would be best to create a separate pantry or section in the refrigerator for yourself.

4 - Read Labels Before Buying Products

When you're on the keto diet, you need to get better in reading labels. Yes, this can be tricky, as there are plenty terms in those labels that you barely understand. Here are some strategies that can help.

Know the many names of sugar

Sugar comes in many names, and you need to know about all these to ensure that you're not side tracked.

- Brown sugar
- White sugar
- Barley malt syrup
- Agave nectar
- Brown rice syrup
- Beet sugar
- Cane crystals
- Cane juice crystals
- Cane sugar
- Coconut sugar
- Coconut palm sugar
- Dehydrated cane juice
- Invert sugar
- Corn sweetener
- Dextrose
- Dextrin
- Evaporated cane juice
- Fruit juice concentrate
- Fructose
- High-fructose corn syrup
- Glucose
- Honey
- Lactose
- Malt syrup
- Corn syrup
- Corn syrup solids
- Treacle
- Maltodextrin
- Maltose
- Molasses
- Turbinado Sugar
- Maple syrup
- Palm sugar
- Raw sugar
- Xylose
- Rice syrup
- Saccharose
- Sorghum or sorghum syrup
- Syrup
- Sucrose

Be careful of sugar-free labels

Some products are labeled as sugar-free, but would actually contain sugar alcohols, which are just as bad.

Examples of sugar alcohols are:

- Maltitol
- Sorbitol
- Xylitol
- Isomalt
- Hydrogenated starch hydrolysates

Stay away from partially hydrogenated oils

Partially hydrogenated oils are trans fats. Avoid any food product that lists this as one of its ingredients.

5 - Buy in Bulk Quantities

Buying in bulk can help you save money when shopping for keto food. But it doesn't mean you have to buy everything in bulk when you go to the grocery.

What you need to do is to plan your menu for the week, and list down all the ingredients that you will be needing. For those that have long shelf life, and those that you will be needing more of, you can buy these in bulk. For example, if most of your dishes require eggs, then you can buy in dozen or in tray instead of per piece.

6 - Drink Lots of Water Is Very Important

As it has been repeated a number of times in this book, drinking water is a must for all keto dieters. Again, this benefits the body in plenty ways.

Since the keto diet is a natural diuretic, doing this will prevent you from getting dehydrated, which is a common side effect of the keto diet. Strive to drink at least eight glasses of water each day.

7 - Be Aware of Alcohol Consumption

In the previous chapter, it was mentioned that alcohol is not allowed in the keto diet. However, we cannot deny the fact that there would be some people who would not be able to give up alcohol, at least that easily.

Here's a list of a few alcoholic beverages that you can occasionally enjoy while on the keto diet:

- Champagne
- Dry sparkling wine
- Red wine
- White wine
- Whiskey
- Dry martini

These alcoholic beverages are only to be consumed once in a while such as when you're attending a party or going out with your friends. Drink one glass per occasion. Do not consume more than twice a week.

8 - Don't Be Afraid to Ask Advice From Others

Most of what you need to know to get started and achieve success with the keto diet can be found in this book. However, there may still be areas that we were not able to cover, especially those that are unique to your personal circumstances.

For example, if you have a pre-existing medical condition, it is imperative that you consult a doctor first before starting this diet.

Now if you are unsure of your diet plan, or you are confident with your menu planning skills, do not hesitate to enlist the help of a professional dietician or nutritionist.

9 – Must Be Patient and Consistent

As with any other diet program that's safe and effective, the ketogenic diet does not provide instant success.

Expect that there will be problems, challenges and hurdles along the way. This is why, you need to be patient throughout the journey to be able to reach your goals.

If there are times that you feel like you want to give up, remember your objectives—why you started this in the first place, and for sure, this will give you the motivation you need to go on.

Another important virtue is consistency. You will not achieve success in the keto diet if you follow it one day and forget all about it the next day. You need to be consistent and follow the rules to the dot.

10 - Maintain a Food Journal

Maintaining a food journal makes it easier for you to track your progress, and determine which foods might be hindering your success.

Take note of all the ingredients that you eat during the day, including the portions and sizes. Yes, this takes a lot of time and effort but at some point, you will realize that this makes things a lot easier and more efficient.

11 - Use Proper Vitamins and Mineral

Eliminating certain types of foods from your diet will also mean a decline in the vitamins and minerals that you're taking in. To counter the effects of nutritional deficiency, it's a good idea to take the right types of supplements.

Here's a list of the vitamins and minerals that you should consider taking a supplement of:

- **Sodium** – 3,000 to 5,000 mg per day
- **Potassium** – 3,000 mg per day
- **Magnesium** – 500 mg per day
- **Calcium** – 1,000 to 1,200 mg per day
- **Vitamin D** – 1,000 IU for every 25 pounds of body weight
- **Vitamin A** – 0.7 to 0.9 mg per day
- **Omega 3 fatty acids** – 3000 mg fish oil per day

12 - Join Some Social Groups

Expect to experience numerous challenges and problems during your ketogenic journey. One of the things that can help is joining social groups.

When you join social groups, whether online or offline, you're going to meet other people who are experiencing the same challenges as you, and who are going through their own pains and hardships. This will make you feel that you are not alone in this journey.

Also, in these social groups, you will find many inspiring success stories that will show you that this is doable. It will make you see that if others can do it, so can you.

Here are a few examples of social groups that you can join online:

- Ketosis & The Ketogenic Community (https://www.facebook.com/ketogenic/)
- Ketogenic Diet (Recipes & Meal Prep) (https://www.facebook.com/groups/ketodietforbeginners/?ref=br_rs)
- Ketogenic Lifestyle (https://www.facebook.com/groups/1746294368990127/?ref=br_rs)
- Ketogenic Diet for Beginners (https://www.facebook.com/groups/losefatwithcat/?ref=br_rs)

13 - Manage Social Outings

Eating out in restaurants is not the only challenge for the keto dieter. There are many social functions and gatherings that will prove to be a challenge as well.

If you're a keto dieter attending a social gathering, and you keep refusing foods that are being served to you, the host (and other guests) will think that you're either rude or weird.

So this doesn't happen, here are what you can do:

- **Explain to the hosts your situation** – When you confirm your attendance to the hosts, inform them that you've just started out on a ketogenic diet. This way, they won't be surprised (or offended) when they see that you now have different food preferences.
- **Eat a snack before going to the party** – This will prevent you from overeating, and still allow you to enjoy the gathering.
- **Focus on other activities** – The food is only one part of the party. There are many activities that you can do there aside from filling yourself with food. Mingle with other guests, catch up with friends you haven't seen for a long time, strut your stuff on the dance floor, engage in the activities available, and so on.
- **Skip the event** – If you are not comfortable going to the event for whatever reason that you have, you don't have to force yourself.

14 - Come Up with a Suitable Reward System

Many things can cause you to lose motivation and get sidetracked during your diet. But if you come up with a reward system, you will be able to get that motivation back.

First, you need to establish tangible goals. Then for each goal that you accomplish, reward yourself with something that you want so badly.

The reward can be a new book that you've been wanting to read or a movie date with your friends. It should not be food-related as this will defeat the purpose of your dieting.

Chapter 6: Important Dos and Don'ts of Keto Diet

Learning about what you should and should not do on a keto diet can spell difference between getting results and falling off track. So keep this list in mind, as it is sure to come in handy at one point in your journey to a keto lifestyle.

Dos

1. Do Increase Your Protein Intake

Since the keto diet is low-carb, your body needs to get energy in another way. This is where protein comes in. By increasing your protein intake, your body is able to break down proteins for energy.
To get enough protein, make sure two or three of your daily meals include one or more high-quality protein sources.
Your best options for minimal fat and calorie are poultry, beef, pork, offal, fish and shellfish.
So make room in your diet for white-meat chicken, duck, pheasant, quail, ground beef or pork, steak, pork chops, ham, tenderloin, goat, veal and turkey. Get your seafood fix with wild-caught cod, halibut, salmon, trout, tuna, snapper, mahi-mahi, flounder, mackerel, catfish, clams, crab, lobster, mussels, oysters, squid and scallops. Try out organ meats like tongue, kidney, liver and heart.
You could also add egg whites to your meals. Or whip up a sauce or dressing or even a shake and then mix in low-carb, unflavored protein powder.
If your meals need some extra fat, you can get protein from bacon and sausage (should not be cured in sugar), whole eggs (preferably free-range), high-protein cheese (cheddar, mozzarella and parmesan) and nut butters (almond, macadamia and peanut).
Just don't overdo it. The recommended levels per pound of lean body mass vary depending on your lifestyle or goal: 0.6g to 0.8g if you're sedentary, 0.8g to 1.0g if you're active, and 1.0g to 1.2g if muscle gain is a priority.

2. Do Increase Sodium Intake

With salt, less is not always better. If you were on a high-carb diet, then yes, you need to minimize your intake. But with a low-carb program such as the keto diet, you actually need to up your salt intake.
For one, your body will be excreting more salt. And you will be cutting out sodium-processed foods.

Low blood sodium levels can hamper a number of physiological functions. It could, for instance, lead to electrolyte imbalance, which many believe is the culprit behind keto flu.

Keto flu is a condition common among those who transition to a keto diet, and typical symptoms include headaches, light-headedness, fatigue and in some cases constipation.

To avoid or counteract this, it is important to replenish the sodium that your body loses with extra salt. The target, according to some experts, is 2g to 4g of sodium per day.

The simplest way to go about this is by incorporating more salt in your food, manually or through salted butter or bullion. You can, for instance, sprinkle Himalayan sea salt (also called pink salt) on your meals or even in your water.

It also helps to drink a cup of organic bone broth daily, eat sodium-rich vegetables such as celery and cucumbers, munch on salted macadamia nuts, or have bacon for breakfast.

3. Do Learn From Successful Keto Dieters

To increase your chances of pulling it off, consider reading up on keto-diet success stories or on guides from those who have "been there, done that."

This kind of research can help you start off on the right track, if you're a newbie, or stay on track, if you're struggling because you aren't seeing results or are finding it hard to adjust and cope with the changes.

Through first-hand accounts of keto dieters, you can learn what it's really like to make the switch. And you can prepare for the challenges that lie ahead along with the demands of the diet.

Looking into how the diet worked for others, and how their lives have changed for the better, can also provide you the inspiration and motivation you need to keep going, in case you're thinking about giving up.

Plus, their practical tips are almost always worth a try. You can find everything from how to avoid the usual pitfalls to tricks for curbing cravings to tried-and-tested recipes and the most keto-friendly products.

Who else would tell you that Omega-3 is a must, that cast-iron pans make for tastier meals, that lemon water comes in handy, that dark chocolate chips can save the day, and that toasted coconut flakes could be your go-to cereal? Keto-fans may just hold the answers.

4. Do Track Your Progress

There are different methods to track your progress on a keto diet.

One is to keep a journal of your keto journey. Take notes daily or at least on a regular basis. Write about the dietary changes you made and how you are feeling—physically and mentally. You can even rate your mood, mental clarity or energy on a scale of 1 to 10. And don't forget to record your ketone levels and any specific results in terms of your weight and body measurements. All this can help you (and any healthcare professional you're consulting with) figure out what works best for you.

Take measurements of your bust, calves, hips, thighs and waist at the beginning and end of each month. This may be more effective and accurate than the scale, as you could be losing fat and inches but not dropping the pounds.

You can also try on clothes that fit you tightly before you began the diet or check a few weeks after if you are a size smaller, garment-wise.

Or you could pose in the same clothing and angle for before-and-after photos: the "before" photo on day one and the "after" photos on days 20, 40 and 60.

And if you want to monitor metrics, invest in a body-fat analyzer. You can use this and a corresponding app to conduct regular hydrostatic body-fat testing and to track everything from your body weight, fat, water and mass to your BMI, protein level, BMR and metabolic age.

5. Do Keep Your Body Hydrated

With the keto diet, you need to make a conscious effort to stay hydrated.

The keto diet has a natural diuretic effect, with your body excreting more water than it normally does. So you end up losing lots of electrolytes and fluid, especially when you're starting out.

If you don't replenish those electrolytes and drink up, dehydration follows and could result in keto flu. It could also impede your progress since your body will be storing as much fat as it can.

Your best source of hydration is water, plenty of it. Still or sparkling water is fine. What's important is that you drink water constantly so that you drink almost a gallon a day or at least the amount (ounces) that is equivalent to half your body weight (pounds). Adding a squeeze of lime, orange or lemon helps, if you prefer your water flavored. And if you find yourself sweating extra due to the heat or post-workout, make sure to drink even more.

Your other options include chicken or bone broth (rich in nutrients and vitamins and can be very energizing), coffee and herbal tea (black or green), coconut or almond milk (unsweetened), and sports drinks (with stevia or sucralose).

Don'ts

1. Don't Eat Fast Food

Steer clear of fast food as much as possible. While you can eat out and still stick to your diet, you need to mindful about where you dine.

Fast-food outlets are notorious for serving food with plenty of preservatives and chemicals. You could order a burger without the bun, but the burger patty may still contain fillers and added salts. Sometimes even their "healthy" dishes have hidden carbs and sugars. The salads, for instance, usually use refined sugar and unsaturated oils. Plus, a restaurant's definition of healthy rarely matches what is considered healthy under a keto diet.

Eating out might feel like your reward after days of strict keto dieting. But if you don't choose restaurants carefully, it could set you back and all your hard work might go to waste.

The good news is that there chains that cater to low-carb diets. You could ask if they have keto-friendly meat options or request for extra vegetables in place of a high-carb food item.

Or you could search for an all-vegan restaurant that offers more choices that will keep you on track.

Just don't hesitate to ask questions if you are unsure about the food sources or want to know more about a dish's ingredients.

You will need to dine out at some point in your keto journey. Just don't risk your chance of success with fast food, especially when there are other alternatives.

2. Don't Fear Fat

Shying or staying away from fats may feel like the right thing to do when you want to lose weight. But in a keto diet, you actually need fats.

The keto diet is largely fats, with fats accounting for 75 percent of food sources—healthy fats that is. Yes, as long as they're the good kind, fats can boost your energy, help you think clearly and bring you closer to your goal.

The recommend amount is three to four tablespoons of fat per meal.

Among your options are animal fats like bacon, unsalted butter, cheese, ghee, heavy cream and mayonnaise. If there are versions derived from grass-fed animals, go with those.

Plant-based saturated fats work well too, with the list including avocado oil, coconut oil, extra virgin olive oil, MCT oil and vegan mayonnaise.

You can cook with these delicious fats or add them as flavoring or dressing.

Also, when you're buying meat, select fattier cuts of steak, roasts, tenderloin, ham, pork chops, goat, turkey, veal and lamb. Fattier is likewise better when it comes to fish.

And if you are a fan of fresh fruit, make avocados a big part of your diet. These are low-carb and bursting in healthy fats, and you can use them in a variety of recipes.

3. Don't Increase Carb Intake

Your carb intake should be limited when you're on the keto diet. So it's important to measure and monitor just how much carbohydrates you are consuming every day.

The keto carb limit is said to be from 35g to 50g of total carbs per day, although some advocates believe as few as 20 grams daily is ideal.

In terms of net carbs, the recommended limit is generally between 20g and 30g. Net carbs, computed by deducting the grams of total fiber from grams of total carbs, are what most keto dieters use to count carbs.

To stay in ketosis, you need to watch your carb intake and ensure it doesn't go beyond this limit.

So keep an eye out for food with hidden carbs. Examples include breaded meats, chicken wings (with barbecue or buffalo sauce), low-fat yogurt and milk.

You also need to eliminate high-carb sources from your diet, particularly sugary and starchy food such as rice, pasta and bread.

Instead, focus on low-carb alternatives that you can consume many times each day. With vegetables, anything besides corn, large tomatoes and potatoes is acceptable. You can have keto-friendly vegetables multiple times each day along with avocado and nuts.

4. Don't Consume Many Root Vegetables

Vegetables that grow underground are rich in fiber and vitamins A and C. But because some of them are too starchy and carb-heavy, you need to choose your root vegetables carefully and consume them in moderation. Otherwise, with all the glucose being broken down, your body will continue to be a sugar burner and you risk ruining your keto diet.

For starters, cross off the usual suspects—regular and sweet potatoes—from the list. One cup of potatoes contains about 26g of carbs.

Then take note of the root veggies that many do not realize are high in carbs as well: beets, carrots, cassava, Jerusalem artichoke, parsnips, yams and yucca. A one-cup serving of parsnips has 24g of carbs, beets 24g, and carrots 12g.

As for the ones that are not as high-carb but should be eaten occasionally only, you have garlic, onion, spring onion, leek, mushrooms, radishes and winter squash.

Most of these can be used as flavoring (such as onion for soup), so it should be easy to track your consumption and avoid going overboard. But of course, it also helps to pay attention to the number of carbs a particular vegetable has before your incorporate it into your program.

5. Don't Exercise During the First Two Weeks

The first two weeks are a tough time for every keto dieter. This period can take a toll on your body, with some suffering from keto flu.

If you don't exercise regularly but would like to start now that you're on a keto diet, hold it off until after the first two weeks. You won't feel like exercising anyway. With all the changes your body is adapting to, you might actually be too weak to work out.

So slow down and focus on getting through this rough patch. After your body becomes fat-adapted, you might feel more energized and motivated to get back on your feet and become more active. Plus, now that your body is producing ketones efficiently, you can look forward to increased strength, muscle gains and fat loss.

You could, for instance, try high-intensity aerobic exercises. With such routines, your body will be tapping fat as its primary energy source (since carbohydrates are not available). And you can reap the benefits after your first two weeks on this diet.

Of course, there are other types of workouts that suit keto dieters. Just remember not to push too early and too hard. Taking things in stages is a smart move as is sticking to what you feel comfortable with.

Chapter 7: Simple Food Guide of Keto Diet

When you're on the ketogenic diet (or any diet program), grocery shopping can be a lot more challenging.

Each time you'd pick a product, you'd have to think twice, thrice or many times if you can actually buy and consume that product, or if it will ruin your diet program.

To make things easier for you, we've rounded up a list of foods that you can eat and foods that are not allowed.

Foods You Can Eat

If you're wondering which specific types of food are allowed in this diet program, here's a list of what you should eat more often.

1. Fats and Oils

As mentioned in the previous chapters, you'll be getting most of your caloric intake from fats. But take note that you can't just devour whatever fat you get your hands on. You need to be picky, and include in your diet those that will not harm your health.

Basically, there are three types of fat allowed in the ketogenic diet:

- **Saturated fat** – Coconut oil, lard, ghee and butter
- **Monounsaturated fat** – Olive oil, macadamia nut oil, avocado oil
- **Polyunsaturated fat** – Fatty fish (wild salmon, trout, tuna), meat protein, non-hydrogenated animal fat

Other good sources of healthy fat:

- Tallow
- Egg yolk
- Brazil nuts
- Mayonnaise
- Cocoa butter
- Coconut butter
- Avocado
- MCT oil

When using vegetable oils such as olive oil or soybean oil, always go for the cold-pressed options. If you are going to cook in high heat, it's better to use oils with higher smoke points such as ghee and coconut oil.

2. Protein

Protein is also a vital part of the ketogenic diet. Consuming too little or too much can wreak havoc to your diet program.

When looking for protein sources, here are some key points to keep in mind:

- Go for grass-fed and pasture-raised meat

- Choose darker meat than white meat
- Be wary of hidden sugars and additives in sausages and cured meat
- Select fattier cuts of meat such as rib eye

Preferred protein sources:
- **Fish** – Cod, flounder, salmon, tuna, catfish, halibut, mahi-mahi, mackerel, snapper
- **Seafood** – Oysters, crabs, mussels, clams, lobster, scallops, squid
- **Eggs** – Free-range chicken, duck or turkey eggs
- **Beef** – Steak, stew met, ground beef, roasts
- **Pork** – Pork chops, pork tenderloin, pork loin
- **Poultry** – Chicken, quail, duck, wild game
- **Offal/organ** – Animal liver, heart, tongue, kidney
- **Other meat** – Goat, lamb, veal
- **Cured meat** – Bacon, sausage, ham (choose those that do not contain sugar or nitrates)
- **Nut butter** – Almond butter, macadamia nut butter

3. Vegetables and Fruits

Vegetables are essential in the keto diet. However, you need to limit intake of those that are high in carbohydrates.

Here are those that should be included in your choices:

- Broccoli
- Cauliflower
- Radishes
- White cabbage
- Green cabbage
- Brussels sprouts
- Zucchini
- Bok choy
- Kale
- Cucumbers
- Olives
- Green beans
- Mushrooms
- Turnips
- Asparagus
- Summer squash
- Bamboo shoots
- Artichoke hearts
- Celery
- Eggplant
- Okra
- Garlic
- Bell pepper

When it comes to fruits, your choices are limited. Fruits are high in sugar, which is the carbohydrate that you'd want to steer clear of when you're on a keto diet.

But you can still eat a few types such as the ones enumerated below:

- Avocado
- Blackberries
- Blueberries
- Raspberries
- Strawberries

4. Dairy Products

Keto dieters are allowed to consume dairy products, but are encouraged to choose raw and organic products. It's important to choose full fat dairy products over those that are low or free of fat.

Here's a list of the dairy products that you can consume under the keto diet program:

- Greek yogurt
- Heavy whipping cream
- Cream cheese
- Sour cream
- Fresh cream
- Cottage cheese
- Brie
- Mozzarella
- Monterey Jack
- Colby
- Mascarpone
- Cheddar
- Parmesan
- Feta
- Swiss cheese

5. Nuts and Seeds

Nuts and seeds are a great source of healthy fat and protein. However, they also contain omega 6 fatty acids, so it's imperative not to eat too much of these.

Nuts and seeds allowed on the keto diet:

- Brazil nuts
- Pecans
- Macadamia nuts
- Walnuts
- Almonds
- Hazel nuts
- Pine nuts

6. Beverages

One of the many things that you have to know about the keto diet is that it is a natural diuretic, which is why dehydration is a common side effect, particularly for those in the initial stage. This makes it imperative to drink at least eight glasses of water a day.

Now what about other drinks and beverages?

Here's a list of what are allowed:

- Broth
- Coffee
-
- Tea
- Coconut milk
- Almond milk

7. Herbs, Spices, Condiments & Sauces

For most people, this is where things get a little tricky. Many are not aware that some spices actually contain carbs. One may not have any idea that he's loading up on carbs just by spicing up his dish. Enumerated below are the herbs and spices that you can use while under this diet:

- Basil
- Cayenne pepper
- Cinnamon
- Chili powder
- Oregano
- Cumin
- Parsley
- Thyme
- Rosemary
- Cilantro
- Salt
- Pepper
- Ketchup
- Mustard
- Hot sauce
- Sauerkraut
- Relish
- Mayonnaise
- Horseradish
- Salad dressing
- Worcestershire sauce

Just make sure that the sauces or condiments that you use do not contain any hidden carbohydrates.

8. Sweeteners

Since sugar is a major no-no in the ketogenic diet program, experts have come up with a list of alternatives that are safe to take in:

- Stevia
- Sucralose
- Erythritol
- Monk fruit
- Swerve

What You Should Avoid

As for foods to avoid, you'd want to stay away from the following:

1. Carbs

Carbohydrates are not allowed in the ketogenic diet for the simple reason that it prevents burning of fat.

Below, you'll find a list of high carb foods that you need to avoid:

- **Grains** – Rice, wheat, barley, oats, rye, corn, quinoa, millet, bulgur, sorghum, amaranth, buckwheat, sprouted grains, and all pasta, breads and crackers made from these grains
- **Beans and legumes** – Kidney beans, chickpeas, lentils, black beans, green peas, lima beans, pinto beans, great northern beans, white beans, black eyed peas, black cannellini beans, fava beans
- **Fruits** – Bananas, apples, pineapple, papaya, oranges, grapes, mangoes, tangerines, all fruit juices, all fruit syrups, all fruit concentrates
- **Starchy vegetables** – Potatoes, sweet potatoes, yams, carrots, peas, yucca, corn, tomatoes
- **Sugars** – Brown sugar, white sugar, cane sugar, raw sugar, honey, agave nectar, maple syrup, turbinado sugar, high fructose corn syrup

2. Protein

Not all protein sources are to be avoided. In fact, some of them have been listed in the foods that are allowed.

But to make sure you stay in ketosis, do not consume the following:

- Milk and low fat dairy products (low fat yogurt, fat free butter substitute, low fat cream cheese, evaporated skim milk, low fat whipped cream)
- Grain fed meats
- Factory-farmed fish and pork
- Processed meat that contain nitrates

3. Fats and Oils

It's a must to avoid processed vegetable oils that will not only ruin your diet but also harm your health:

- Soybean oil
- Canola oil
- Corn oil
- Grapeseed oil
- Sunflower oil
- Peanut oil
- Safflower oil
- Sesame oil

4. Beverages

It's best to keep yourself hydrated with water and other drinks that are keto friendly.
As much as possible, steer clear of the following:

- **Alcohol** – Beers, wines, cocktails, flavored liquers
- **Sugary drinks** – Soda, diet soda, fruit juices, fruit smoothies, coffee or tea with milk or sugar, sweetened milk

5. Processed food products

Whether you're on the keto diet or not, you should always make it a point to avoid processed foods. These are loaded with chemicals, preservatives, sugars, and trans fats that can harm the health in more ways than one.
Just a few examples of processed food products to avoid include:

- **Commercially baked goods** – Cookies, cakes
- **Sweet treats** – Candies, ice cream
- **Canned goods and instant foods** – Cup noodles, rice packet meals, canned vegetables and meat products
- **"Junk food"** – Potato chips, corn chips, buttered or sweetened popcorn
- **Fast Food** – French fries, burgers, pizza and other foods from fast food chains

6. Sweeteners

Certain artificial sweeteners have been found to negatively affect blood sugar levels. These include:

- Equal
- Acesulfame
- Aspartame
- Saccharin

Knowing which foods to eat and avoid is one of the first steps towards the ketogenic diet success.

Chapter 8: Top 4 Frequently Asked Questions

Question 1. Why Does the Keto Diet Help to Lose Weight Faster?

With the keto diet, your weight will drop quickly the first week. The usual weight loss during this adjustment phase is from 2 to 7 pounds, although some lose up to 10 pounds.

Most of that will be water weight. This is because your body, in response to your reduced carb intake, won't burn fat right away. Instead it will start by burning all your glycogen reserves. Between 2g and 3g of water is bound to each gram of glycogen, making for drastic water-weight loss. Plus, after your glycogen reserves are depleted, water required to store glycogen is eliminated.

Your body will then transition into a fat-burning mode, and for the second to fourth weeks you can expect to lose one to two pounds per week.

This is referred to as the adaptation phase, as your body is getting used to tapping fat—instead of carbs—as your main fuel source.

For regular and stable weight loss, you need to keep your daily net carb intake below 20g and monitor your calories.

It also helps that there's more fat and protein than carbs in your body. Fat and protein leave you feeling full longer than carbs do, so you won't be hungry as often.

By the fourth week or so, you will be fat-adapted and can continue to loss one to two pounds each week, depending on the calories you consume and how much physical activity you engage in. At this point, you probably won't have carb cravings anymore and your improved energy will allow you to step up your workouts.

Just keep in mind that the rate and amount of weight loss vary with each person and is determined by a range of factors, including your age, metabolism, activity level, how much body fat you have and how committed you are to the keto diet.

Question 2. What Should I Prepare before Following the Ketogenic Diet?

Here are some ways you can prepare for and successfully ease into the keto diet.

Do your homework

Read up on the keto diet. There are tons on online articles and guides that you can easily access plus a number of books that make for great reference materials.

Your research should cover the basics of the keto diet—what it is, what it's like, what it requires, what you can expect. Also look up recommended foods, keto-friendly alternatives for your favorites, and tried-and-tested recipes and meal plans.

Do the math

To be able to reach and maintain ketosis, you need to restrict your net carb intake. And to be able to choose foods that will keep you within your limit, you need to learn how to calculate net carbs early on.

The net carb equation is pretty simple. It involves just two values: total carbohydrate and dietary fiber. Both these appear on standard U.S. nutrition labels.

To determine a food item's net carb content (per serving), just subtract the dietary fiber content from the total carbohydrate content.

If the number of grams you get is too close to, exceeds or is more than half of your net carb limit, then it's not keto-friendly.

Clear your kitchen

Check your refrigerator and pantry for non-ketogenic foods and keep them out of reach. You'll have hard-to-resist carb cravings when you start out, and you might be tempted to give into those cravings if you can easily get your hands on bread, chips, pasta, cereal, corn, rice, cookies, ice cream, chocolate, candy, honey, maple syrup and sugary drinks.

In addition to these, you need to steer clear of beans, apples, oranges, bananas, yams and potatoes, as these are all carb-heavy.

Stock up

Shop for and fill your kitchen with food that's keto-friendly. Begin with the staples: butter, coconut oil, fatty meats (beef, fish, pork and poultry), eggs, leafy greens and other low-carb vegetables (cauliflower, broccoli).

Also get some fruits (avocados, blackberries, raspberries), nuts and seeds (walnuts, macadamias, sunflower seeds), kale chips, high-fat salad dressing and cream, and hard cheeses. It pays to have sweeteners (monk fruit, erythritol, stevia) too, as these will help keep you away from bread and sugary items.

Remember to hit the aisles only after eating a small fatty meal. Being satiated, rather than starved, in a grocery store reduces the likelihood that you would buy something that's not on your list. Or simply shop online instead.

To prevent overeating and keep your calorie count low, go for less variety in terms of the foods you stock at a given time. Also, store your favorites in places that are not quickly accessible or within view.

Plan meals

Well-planned meals will set you off on the right track, and you won't have to waste time worrying or stressing about what to have for your next meal.

The key to successful meal planning: your macros. You need to have the right ratio of fats (75 percent), protein (20 percent) and carbs (5 percent) every day, and you can use online macro calculators to determine the required number of grams for each.

Search for recipes based on your calculations and prepare your week's meal plan accordingly.

Make small changes

Prepare for the demands of the keto diet by gradually reducing carbs and increasing fats.

- When you dine out, skip the burger bun and have it replaced with lettuce. And instead of having rice or potatoes with your meal, request for green veggies.
- Use more oil when you cook.
- Add salt to your meals.
- Begin taking supplements (mainly for magnesium, potassium and sodium).

Tell your family and friends

Explain to your loved ones what the keto diet is all about, why you want to try it, and how this will change your meals and eating habits. This way, they can provide you support rather than set you back.

Choose a start date

The date should be on a week where your schedule is clear—no deadlines to beat, no obligations to attend to, no planned trips, parties or lunch/dinner dates. The whole week has to be non-stressful so you can rest well during the adjustment phase.

Question 3. Should I have a Lifelong Ketogenic Diet?

While the keto diet has grown popular in recent years, there aren't research studies yet that support its effectiveness as a lifelong diet.
But many believe it is a short-term fix, a temporary diet you go on for four to six months if your primary goal is weight control. The good news is you can expect sustained fat loss. If you are able to maintain healthy eating habits, chances are you won't regain the weight you lost.
Some advocates feel staying on the keto diet is beneficial if you have diabetes, anxiety and neurological disorders, commonly experience brain fog, or need the continued energy boost.

Question 4. Can I Follow Ketogenic Diet If I am In Vegan/Vegetarian Diet?

Yes. The keto diet can be adapted to fit a vegetarian's lifestyle. This version, referred to as the vegetarian ketogenic diet, is designed around plant-based meals but incorporates principles of the keto diet. So it lets vegetarians enjoy the health benefits of ketosis without drastically changing their lifestyle.
The vegetarian ketogenic diet excludes all kinds of animal flesh: meat, poultry and fish. The only animal products allowed are eggs and dairy.
The list of acceptable foods also includes non-starchy vegetables like leafy greens, low-sugar fruits, healthy fats, and plant-based proteins such as nuts, seeds, nutritional yeast, tempeh, spirulina and natto.

Chapter 9: Keto Diet Appetizer & Breakfast Recipes

Chicken Enchilada Dip

Serves: 2
Preparation time: 5 minutes
Cooking Time: 1 hour
Ingredients:

1 lb rotisserie chicken, pre-cooked and shredded

4 oz pepper jack cheese, shredded

5 oz enchilada sauce

4 oz cream cheese, softened

Instructions:

Combine all the ingredients in the crockpot. Mix thoroughly.

Cover and cook for 1 hours on low.

Nutritional Value:

Calories: 172, Fat: 19.7 g, Net carbs: 5.8 g, Protein: 15 g

Serving suggestions: Top with sliced green onions.

BBQ Bison Phyllo Bites

Serves: 2
Preparation time: 15 minutes
Cooking Time: 12 hours
Ingredients:

1 lb bison brisket

6 oz miniature phyllo dough shells

2 1/2 tsp Worcestershire sauce

1 tbsp cheddar cheese, shredded

1 3/4 tsp barbecue sauce

Instructions:

Except for the dough shells, combine all ingredients in the crockpot. Season with salt and pepper, 1 tsp vinegar, 1 clove of garlic and spices of choice.

Add 1/4 cup of water.

Cover and cook for 12 hours on low.

Arrange phyllo doughs on a baking pan and divide the bison among them.

Bake for 10 minutes at 375 F.

Nutritional Value:

Calories: 119, Fat: 3.5 g, Net carbs: 5.6 g, Protein: 13.9 g

Serving suggestions: Top with sour cream and fresh cilantro.

Spinach Artichoke Dip

Serves: 2
Preparation time: 15 minutes
Cooking Time: 12 hours
Ingredients:
3 oz spinach, thawed and drained
7 oz artichoke hearts, drained and quartered
1/8 cup parmesan cheese, grated
1/4 cup mozzarella cheese, shredded
1/8 cup milk
Instructions:
Place all ingredients in the crockpot. Add garlic and pepper to taste. Mix thoroughly.
Cover and cook for 2 hours on high, stirring occasionally.
Nutritional Value:
Calories: 126, Fat: 12.9 g, Net carbs: 4.2 g, Protein: 9.7 g
Tip: If dip is too thick, add milk until desired consistency is acquired.

Bacon-Wrapped Smokies

Serves: 2
Preparation time: 15 minutes
Cooking Time: 6 hours
Ingredients:
1/2 lb sliced bacon, cut into thirds
7 oz beef cocktail wieners
Instructions:
Wrap each wiener with bacon and secure each one with a toothpick.
Place them in the crockpot.
Cover and cook for 6 hours on low.
Nutritional Value:
Calories: 163, Fat: 5.3 g, Net carbs: 5.4 g, Protein: 6.5 g
Tip: Use a liner in crockpot to keep cleaning easier.

Hot Onion Dip

Serves: 8
Preparation time: 30 minutes
Ingredients:
1 cup onion, grated
8 oz. cream cheese
1 cup full fat mayo
1 cup Swiss cheese, grated
Preparation:
1) Combine all the ingredients in a baking dish.
2) Cover the dish with foil.
3) Pour 1 cup of water into the Instant Pot.
4) Place a steamer rack inside the pot.
5) Put the baking dish on top of the rack.
6) Cover the pot.
7) Set it to manual.
8) Cook at high pressure for 15 minutes.
9) Release the pressure naturally.

Serving Suggestion: Serve with vegetable sticks, pork rinds or low carb crackers.

Tip: You can also blend the ingredients in a food processor to shorten preparation time.

Nutritional Information Per Serving:

Calories 271, Total Fat 23.5g, Saturated Fat 10.1g, Cholesterol 51mg, Sodium 319mg , Total Carbohydrate 6.8g, Dietary Fiber 0.3g, Total Sugars 2.7g, Protein 6.2g, Potassium 68mg

Short Ribs with Creamy Mushroom Sauce

Serves: 2
Preparation time: 5 minutes
Cooking Time: 6 hours
Ingredients:
1/8 cup beef broth
1/2 cup white mushrooms
1/2 lb beef short ribs, browned
3.4 oz softened cream cheese
Directions:
Prepare seasonings: 1/4 tsp garlic powder, 1/4 tsp salt, and 1/4 tsp pepper.
Add seasonings to beef broth, cream cheese and mushrooms in a crock-pot.
Put the short ribs on top.
Cover and cook on low for 6 hours. Mix every hour.
Nutritional Value:
Calories: 365, Fat: 33g, Net Carbs: 1g, Protein: 13g, Sodium: 422mg, Potassium: 295mg

Chuck Roast with Mustard Sauce

Serves: 2   **Preparation time:** 10 minutes   **Cooking Time:** 4 hours

Ingredients:

3/4 lb chuck roast cut in 1-inch cubes

1/2 chopped celery stalk

1 oz heavy cream

1 tbsp yellow mustard

Directions:

Prepare the seasonings: 0.25 tsp garlic powder, 0.25 tsp salt and 0.13 diced onion. Mix them with the cream and mustard in the crock-pot. Mix thoroughly.

Add the chopped celery stalk and the chuck roast cubes in the crock-pot. Mix.

Cover and cook for 4 hours on high.

Nutritional Value:

Calories: 364, Fat: 25g, Protein: 33g, Net Carbs: 1g, Sodium: 506mg, Potassium 623mg

Tip: Cook in crock-pot in 6 hours for medium heat or 8 hours in low heat.

Beef & Broccoli

Serves: 2   **Preparation time:** 10 minutes   **Cooking Time:** 6 hours

Ingredients:

1/2 head broccoli cut in 1-inch pieces

1/2 red bell pepper cut in 1-inch pieces

1/3 cup liquid aminos

1/2 cup beef broth

1 lb flank steak cut in 1 to 2-inch cubes

Directions:

Prepare the seasonings: 1 1/2 tbsp of chosen sweetener, 1/2 tsp grated ginger, 1 1/2 minced garlic cloves and salt to taste.

Add beed broth, aminos and the steak cubes in a crock-pot. Add the seasonings.

Cook for 5 hours on low.

Add the broccoli and bell pepper on top and cook for another hour.

Nutritional Value:

Calories: 430, Fat: 19g, Net Carbs: 3g, Fiber: 1g. Protein 54g

Serving suggestions: Serve over riced cauliflower. For garnishing, sprinkle with sesame seeds

Tip: You can make an arrowroot slurry to thicken the sauce. Mix 1 tablespoon of arrowroot flour with 2 tbsp of cold water and add to the cooked recipe. It contains 1g carb per tablespoon.

Bacon Egg Bites

Serves: 8
Preparation time: 30 minutes
Ingredients:

4 eggs, beaten

¼ cup egg whites, beaten

¼ cup heavy whipping cream

½ cup cottage cheese

4 slices bacon, cooked and crumbled

½ red pepper, chopped

½ green pepper, chopped

1 cup red onion, chopped

1 cup shredded cheddar cheese

Salt and pepper to taste

Preparation:

1) Mix the eggs, egg whites, cream and cottage cheese.
2) Pour 1 cup of water into the Instant Pot.
3) Place a steamer rack inside the pot.
4) Pour the mixture into muffin tins.
5) Place the muffin tins on top of the rack.
6) Top each container with bacon, peppers and onion.
7) Cover the pot.
8) Set it to steam mode.
9) Release the pressure naturally.
10) Top with the cheddar cheese, and season with the salt and pepper before serving.

Serving Suggestion: Serve with low carb or keto crackers.

Tip: To prepare the dish faster, use a blender to mix the eggs, cheese and cream.

Nutritional Information Per Serving:

Calories 358

Total Fat 25.1g

Saturated Fat 12g

Cholesterol 227mg

Sodium 811mg

Total Carbohydrate 6.9g

Dietary Fiber 1.1g

Total Sugars 3g

Protein 25.9g

Potassium 348mg

Avocado & Egg Bites

Serves: 6

Preparation time: 25 minutes

Ingredients:

4 eggs

½ cup Mexican blend cheese

¼ cup heavy cream

½ cup cottage cheese

¼ teaspoon garlic powder

¼ teaspoon chili powder

¼ teaspoon cumin

Salt and pepper to taste

1 cup avocado, chopped

Preparation:

1) Pour 1 cup of water into the Instant Pot.
2) In a bowl, add all the ingredients except the avocado.
3) Pulse in the blender until smooth.
4) Pour the mixture into 4 silicone molds.
5) Place the mold on a steamer rack inside the pot.
6) Secure the lid.
7) Press the steam setting.
8) Set it to 10 minutes.
9) Release the pressure naturally.
10) Top with the chopped avocado.

Serving Suggestion: Sprinkle more cheese on top.

Tip: Skip the chilli powder if you don't like the dish to be spicy.

Nutritional Information Per Serving:

Calories 118

Total Fat 13g

Saturated Fat 6g

Cholesterol 115mg

Sodium 179mg

Total Carbohydrates 1g

Protein 7g

Potassium 101mg

Turkey Sausage, Egg & Cheese

Serves: 6
Preparation time: 20 minutes
Ingredients:
12 eggs, beaten
1 cup almond milk
Salt and pepper to taste
3 cups turkey breakfast sausage
1 onion, diced
2 cups cheddar cheese, shredded
Preparation:
1) In a bowl, mix the eggs, almond milk, salt and pepper.
2) Coat the Instant Pot with cooking spray.
3) Pour the egg mixture into the pot.
4) Arrange a layer of the sausage, onion and cheese on top of the egg mixture.
5) Cover the pot.
6) Press the manual setting.
7) Cook at high pressure for 10 minutes.
8) Release the pressure naturally.

Serving Suggestion: Sprinkle chopped green onion on top.
Tip: Use ham or bacon in place of turkey sausage
Nutritional Information Per Serving:
Calories 377
Total Fat 30.8g
Saturated Fat 19.1g
Cholesterol 367mg
Sodium 364mg
Total Carbohydrate 5.1g
Dietary Fiber 1.3g
Total Sugars 3g
Protein 21.6g
Potassium 287mg

Jalapeno Omelet

Serves: 6
Preparation time: 20 minutes
Ingredients:

Cooking spray
1 cup bacon, chopped
4 jalapeno pepper, seeded and chopped
12 eggs, beaten

¼ cup heavy cream
Salt and pepper to taste
1 cup cheddar cheese, shredded

Preparation:

1) Spray glass jars with oil.
2) Set the Instant Pot to sauté.
3) Cook the bacon until golden crisp.
4) Drain fat and set aside.
5) Add the jalapeno peppers to the pot.
6) Cook for 2 minutes.
7) In a bowl, whisk the eggs, cream, salt and pepper.
8) Fold in the peppers, bacon and cheese.
9) Pour the egg mixture into the glass jars.
10) Place a steamer rack inside the Instant Pot.
11) Pour in 2 cups of water.
12) Put the jars on top of the rack.
13) Cover the jars.
14) Cover the pot.
15) Set it to manual.
16) Cook at high pressure for 7 minutes.
17) Release the pressure naturally.

Serving Suggestion: Garnish top with chopped fresh herbs.

Tip: Cook only for 5 minutes if you want the eggs to be softer.

Nutritional Information Per Serving:

Calories 273
Total Fat 20.9g
Saturated Fat 9.2g
Cholesterol 364mg
Sodium 462mg
Total Carbohydrate 1.8g
Dietary Fiber 0.3g

Total Sugars 1.1g
Protein 19.5g
Potassium 214mg

Chapter 10: Keto Diet Meat Recipes

Butter Beef

Serves: 2   **Preparation time:** 5 minutes   **Cooking Time:** 5 hours

Ingredients:

2 tbsp butter

1/4 envelope dry onion soup mix

3/4 lb beef stew meat, cubed

Directions:

Simply put all the ingredients in the crock-pot. Mix well.

Cover and cook for 4 to 5 hours on high. Stir after the first 2 hours.

Nutritional Value:

Calories: 437, Fat: 34.6g, Net Carbs: 2.2g, Protein: 28g, Cholesterol: 124mg, Sodium: 457mg

Serving suggestion: Served over egg noodles for best results.

Tip: Cook for 8 hours in low. For easier cleanup, a liner can be used in the crock-pot insides.

Ronaldo's Beef Carnitas

Serves: 2   **Preparation time:** 5 minutes   **Cooking Time:** 8 hours

Ingredients:

11 oz chuck roast

1/8 can green chili peppers, chopped

1 tsp chili powder

1/8 tsp dried oregano

1/8 tsp ground cumin

Directions:

Prepare the seasonings: mix all ingredient except the chuck roast. Add salt and pepper to taste.

Rub the mixture generously on the chuck roast and cover with aluminum foil. Put in the crock-pot.

Cover and cook for about 8 hours on low.

Nutritional Value:

Calories: 218, Fat: 13.8g, Net Carbs: 1.4g, Protein: 20.8g, Cholesterol: 70mg, Sodium: 170mg

Serving suggestions: When cooked, it can easily be shredded with forks. It is best served in flour tortillas, possibly with salsa and guacamole.

Mushroom Roast Beef

Serves: 2
Preparation time: 5 minutes
Cooking Time: 9 hours
Ingredients:

1 envelope onion soup mix

1 bottle beer

1 lb sliced fresh mushrooms

1 standing beef rib roast

Directions:

Sprinkle the onion soup mix generously on the beef roast, with added black pepper to taste.

Pour mushrooms on the crock-pot and set the beef roast atop.

Pour the beer all over the slow cooker.

Cover and cook for 9 hours on low

Nutritional Value:

Calories: 388, Fat: 28.1g, Net Carbs: 6.2g, Protein: 24.4g, Cholesterol: 82mg, Sodium: 453mg

Serving suggestions: When cooked, shred meat with two forks.

Tip: For easier cleanup, a liner can be used in the crock-pot insides.

Taco Soup with Beef

Serves: 2
Preparation time: 10 minutes
Cooking Time: 4 hours
Ingredients:

1 cup cream cheese

1 cup cheddar cheese, shredded

1/2 cup tomato puree

2 lb ground beef, sautéed

3 1/2 cup chicken broth

Directions:

Combine everything in a crock-pot. Add salt to taste.

Cover and cook for 4 hours on low.

Nutritional Value:

Calories: 569, Fat: 41.2g, Net Carbs: 4.8g, Protein: 43g

Serving suggestions: For garnish, 2 toasted slices of cheddar cheese can be added. Corianders on top can also add extra flavor.

Tip: To make a thicker soup, simply add cream and cheddar cheese to the soup and stir. Cook for additional 30 minutes.

Pork Chop with Mushrooms

Serves: 4
Preparation time: 60 minutes
Ingredients:

4 pork chops
2 tablespoons butter
2 tablespoons coconut oil, divided
1 cup chicken stock

1 onion sliced
8 oz. mushrooms, chopped
Salt and pepper to taste

Preparation:

1) Season the pork chops with the salt and pepper.
2) Add the butter and half of the coconut oil to the Instant Pot.
3) Set it to sauté.
4) Sear the pork chops for 2 minutes per side.
5) Remove from the pot and set aside.
6) Add the remaining coconut oil.
7) Add the onion and cook for 2 minutes.
8) Add the mushrooms and cook for another 2 minutes.
9) Pour in the chicken stock.
10) Scrape the brown bits using a wooden spoon.
11) Put the pork chops back to the pot.
12) Seal the pot.
13) Set it to manual.
14) Cook at high pressure for 10 minutes.
15) Release the pressure quickly.
16) Remove the pork chops.
17) Press sauté.
18) Add the remaining coconut oil. Cook for 5 minutes.
19) Pour cooking liquid on top of the pork chops before serving.

Serving Suggestion: Serve with fresh green salad.
Tip: Add a sprinkle of dried basil to the pork chops.
Nutritional Information:

Calories 391
Total Fat 32.8g
Saturated Fat 17g
Cholesterol 84mg
Sodium 292mg

Total Carbohydrate 4.6g
Dietary Fiber 1.2g
Total Sugars 2.3g
Protein 20.3g
Potassium 501mg

Chorizo Chili

Serves: 6
Preparation time: 40 minutes
Ingredients:

1 ½ tablespoons olive oil
1 onion, chopped
1 celery stick, cubed
7 oz. chorizo sausage, diced
½ carrot, cubed
1 red chili, diced
3 cloves garlic, diced

2.2 lb. ground beef
3 teaspoons cumin
2 cups canned tomatoes
4 tablespoon tomato paste
1 tablespoon soy sauce
2 bay leaves
Salt to taste

Preparation:

1) Set the Instant Pot to sauté.
2) Add the olive oil.
3) Cook the onion, celery, chorizo, carrot and chilli for 4-5 minutes.
4) Add the garlic, beef and the rest of the ingredients.
5) Mix well.
6) Secure the lid.
7) Press manual mode.
8) Cook at high pressure for 15 minutes.
9) Release the pressure naturally.
10) Season with the salt.

Serving Suggestion: Serve with chopped avocado on the side.
Tip: Add chili powder if you like your dish spicy.
Nutritional Information:

Calories 568
Total Fat 43g
Saturated Fat 12.8g
Cholesterol 176mg
Sodium 554mg
Total Carbohydrate 7.7g
Dietary Fiber 1.8g
Total Sugars 4g
Protein 58.6g

Potassium 1091mg

Tomato Meatballs

Serves: 4

Preparation time: 30 minutes

Ingredients:

1.3 lb. ground beef

1 teaspoon garlic powder

1 teaspoon onion powder

1 teaspoon dried oregano

Salt to taste

2 tablespoons olive oil

1 onion, diced

2 cloves garlic, diced

2 cups canned tomatoes

Preparation:

1) Mix the ground beef, garlic powder, onion powder, oregano and salt in a bowl.
2) Form 8-10 meatballs.
3) Choose the sauté function in the Instant Pot.
4) Add the olive oil, onion and garlic.
5) Cook for 5 minutes, stirring frequently.
6) Add the meatballs.
7) Pour in the tomato sauce.
8) Mix well.
9) Lock the lid in place.
10) Press manual.
11) Cook at high pressure for 5 minutes.
12) Release the pressure naturally.

Serving Suggestion: Serve with cauliflower rice or spaghetti squash.

Tip: Add chili powder if you like your meatballs spicy.

Nutritional Information:

Calories 369

Total Fat 26.5g

Saturated Fat 7.5g

Cholesterol 132mg

Sodium 142mg

Total Carbohydrate 7.8g

Dietary Fiber 2g

Total Sugars 4g

Protein 46.1g

Potassium 873mg

Beef Roast

Serves: 6

Preparation time: 1 hour and 20 minutes

Ingredients:

2 tablespoons olive oil

1 tablespoon butter

4 lb. beef chuck roast

16 oz. jarred pepperoncini peppers, sliced

½ onion, sliced thinly

2 cloves garlic, crushed and minced

1 cup beef broth

1 tablespoon onion powder

1 tablespoon oregano

1 tablespoon parsley

1 teaspoon basil

1 tablespoon garlic salt

Salt and pepper to taste

Preparation:

1) Press the sauté function in the Instant Pot.
2) Add the olive oil and butter.
3) Brown the beef on all sides for 4-6 minutes.
4) Add half of the pepperoncini peppers.
5) Pour in ¼ cup of its juice.
6) Add the onion, garlic, beef broth and the rest of the ingredients.
7) Seal the pot.
8) Set it to manual.
9) Cook at high pressure for 70 minutes.
10) Release the pressure naturally.
11) Shred the meat before serving.
12) Top with the remaining pepperoncini.

Serving Suggestion: Enjoy this dish with buttered corn.

Tip: To save time, you can replace the seasonings with a dry seasoning pack of Italian dressing.

Nutritional Information:

Calories 1177

Total Fat 91.1g

Saturated Fat 35.5g

Cholesterol 317mg

Sodium 336mg

Total Carbohydrate 3.8g

Dietary Fiber 0.8g

Total Sugars 1.3g

Protein 80.6g

Potassium 785mg

Butter Beef

Serves: 6
Preparation time: 1 hour and 15 minutes
Ingredients:
3 lb. beef roast
1 tablespoon olive oil
2 tablespoons ranch dressing seasoning mix
2 tablespoons zesty Italian seasoning mix
1 jar pepper rings
1 stick butter
Preparation:
1) Set the Instant Pot to sauté.
2) Add the olive oil into the pot.
3) Sear the beef roast on all sides.
4) Pour in 4 cups of water.
5) Add the seasonings and pepper rings.
6) Place butter stick on top of the roast.
7) Seal the pot.
8) Set it to manual.
9) Cook at high pressure for 60 minutes.
10) Release the pressure naturally.
11) Slice the beef before serving.

Serving Suggestion: Serve with pureed cauliflower.
Tip: You can also shred the beef using 2 forks.
Nutritional Information:
Calories 582
Total Fat 31.7g
Saturated Fat 15.3g
Cholesterol 243mg
Sodium 402mg
Total Carbohydrate 1.1g
Dietary Fiber 0g
Total Sugars 0.1g
Protein 69g
Potassium 918mg

Chapter 11: Keto Diet Chicken & Poultry Recipes

Crack Chicken

Serves: 2
Preparation time: 15 minutes
Cooking Time: 8 hours
Ingredients:

1 chicken breast
1 packet of Ranch dressing

4 oz cream cheese
2 slices bacon, cooked and crumbled

Instructions:

Put the chicken breast in the crockpot.

Pour the dressing in and add the cream cheese.

Cover and cook for 8 hours on low.

Mix in the crumbled bacon when cooked.

Nutritional Value:

Calories: 410, Fat: 32 g, Net carbs: 4 g, Protein: 28 g

Serving suggestions: Shred the chicken before serving.

Ranch Chicken

Serves: 2
Preparation time: 5 minutes
Cooking Time: 5 hours
Ingredients:

1 chicken breast
1/3 tbsp Ranch seasoning
2 cups broccoli florets

4 slices bacon, cooked and crumbled
1/4 cup mayonnaise

Instructions:

Put the chicken in the crockpot and add the seasoning. Add some shallots to taste.

Cover and cook for 4 hours on low.

Add the broccoli and cook for another hour on low.

When cooked, add the bacon, mayonnaise, 1 tbsp vinegar and salt to taste. Stir well.

Nutritional Value:

Calories: 424, Fat: 23.3 g, Net carbs: 4.8 g, Protein: 39.08 g

Serving suggestions: Shred the chicken before serving.

Salsa Chicken

Serves: 2   **Preparation time:** 15 minutes   **Cooking Time:** 2 hours

Ingredients:

1 chicken breast   1/2 cup shredded cheese

1/2 cup fresh salsa

Instructions:

Lightly grease your crockpot with olive oil.

Place the chicken breast in the crockpot and pour the salsa over it.

Cover and cook for 2 hours on high.

When cook, top with cheese and bake for 15 minutes in a preheated oven to 425 F degrees.

Nutritional Value:

Calories: 398, Fat: 18.3 g, Net carbs: 4.2 g, Protein: 42.9 g

Serving suggestions: Serve with low-carb tortilla or leaf lettuce.

Tip: Garnish with fresh cilantro and full-fat sour cream for extra flavor and fats.

4. Chicken Tikka Masala

Serves: 2

Preparation time: 15 minutes

Cooking Time: 6 hours

Ingredients:

1 lb chicken thighs, de-boned and chopped into   5 oz diced tomatoes

bite-size   1/2 cup heavy cream

3 tsp Garam Masala   1/2 cup coconut milk

Instructions:

Put chicken to crockpot and add grated ginger knob on top. Also add the seasonings: 1 tsp onion powder, 2 minced cloves of garlic, 1 tsp paprika and 2 tsp salt. Mix.

Add tomatoes and coconut oil. Mix.

Cook for 6 hours on low.

When cooked, add heavy cream to thicken the curry.

Nutritional Value:

Calories: 493, Fat: 41.2 g, Net carbs: 5.8 g, Protein: 46 g

Serving suggestions: You can further thicken the curry with 1 tsp guar gum. Top with chopped cilantros for presentation.

Tip: Cook for 3 hours on high.

Lemongrass and Coconut Chicken Drumsticks

Serves: 2   **Preparation time:** 15 minutes   **Cooking Time:** 5 hours

Ingredients:

5 chicken drumsticks, skinless

1 stalk lemongrass, rough bottom removed

1/2 cup coconut milk

1/2 tbsp coconut aminos

Instructions:

Season drumsticks with salt and pepper. Place in the crockpot.

In a blender, mix the lemongrass, coconut milk, coconut aminos, garlic and ginger to taste, 1 tbsp fish sauce and desired spices. Pour the mixture over the drumsticks.

Cover and cook on low for 5 hours.

Nutritional Value:

Calories: 460, Fat: 39.7 g, Net carbs: 4.7 g, Protein: 36 g

Serving suggestions: Top with 1/4 cup fresh scallions.

Tip: This is a sensitive recipe which should not be cooked on high.

Crack Chicken

Serves: 6   **Preparation time:** 20 minutes

Ingredients:

1 cup bone broth

2 lb. chicken tenders

Salt and pepper to taste

12 oz. cream cheese

8 oz. bacon, cooked and crumbled

½ cup cheddar cheese

Preparation:

1) Pour the bone broth into the Instant Pot. Season the chicken with the salt and pepper.
2) Add the chicken and cream cheese into the pot. Cover the pot. Set it to manual.
3) Cook at high pressure for 10 minutes. Release the pressure naturally.
4) Stir in the bacon and cheddar cheese.
5) Cover the pot and wait for the cheese to melt before serving.

Serving Suggestion: Serve with any low carb grilled vegetables.

Tip: If you're going to use chicken breasts, increase cooking time to 12 minutes.

Nutritional Information:

Calories 440, Total Fat 38.4g, Saturated Fat 8g, Cholesterol 181.3mg, Sodium 396.7mg

Total Carbohydrate 3.5g, Dietary Fiber 0g, Sugars 2.2g, Protein 41.1g

Whole Chicken

Serves: 6-8

Preparation time: 50 minutes

Ingredients:

1 whole chicken

Garlic salt to taste

Pepper to taste

3 teaspoons dried rosemary

3 tablespoons coconut oil

Preparation:

1) Pour 1 cup of water into the Instant Pot.
2) Place a steamer rack inside.
3) Coat the chicken with garlic salt, pepper and rosemary.
4) Put the chicken on top of the steamer rack.
5) Cover the pot.
6) Set it to manual.
7) Cook at high pressure for 20 minutes.
8) Release the pressure naturally.

Serving Suggestion: Serve with grilled vegetables.

Tip: Let the chicken cool for 1 to 2 minutes before slicing and serving.

Nutritional Information Per Serving:

Calories 429

Total Fat 21.2g

Saturated Fat 9.9g

Cholesterol 173mg

Sodium 169mg

Total Carbohydrate 0.1g

Dietary Fiber 0g

Total Sugars 0g

Protein 56.3g

Potassium 474mg

Turkey & Veggies

Serves: 6

Preparation time: 20 minutes

Ingredients:

1 tablespoon olive oil

1 tablespoon butter

1 lb. ground turkey

1 ½ tablespoons chili paste

1 onion, chopped

2 teaspoons garlic, minced

1 ½ cups bell pepper, chopped

1 cup zucchini, chopped

1 cup vegetable broth

1 cup tomato sauce

14 oz. canned tomatoes

Preparation:

1) Choose the sauté setting in the Instant Pot.
2) Pour in the olive oil.
3) Add the ground turkey.
4) Cook until brown.
5) Add the rest of the ingredients.
6) Mix well.
7) Secure the lid.
8) Set it to manual.
9) Cook at high pressure for 8 minutes.
10) Do a quick pressure release.

Serving Suggestion: Enjoy this dish with a cup of cauliflower rice.

Tip: Try using fire-roasted tomatoes for a more intense flavor.

Nutritional Information Per Serving:

Calories 156

Total Fat 12g

Saturated fat 7g

Cholesterol 41mg

Sodium 169mg

Total Carbohydrates 2g

Dietary Fiber 3g

Sugars 6g

Protein 20g

Potassium 644mg

Chicken Tikka Masala

Serves: 6

Preparation time: 30 minutes

Ingredients:

2 tablespoons butter

1 onion, chopped

½ bell pepper, chopped

3 cloves garlic, minced

1 teaspoon fresh ginger, grated

1 teaspoon turmeric

1 teaspoon cumin

2 teaspoons garam masala

1 teaspoon coriander

¼ teaspoon cayenne pepper

Salt to taste

15 oz. canned diced tomatoes

½ cup coconut milk

2 lb. chicken breast

Preparation:

1) Select the sauté mode in the Instant Pot.
2) Add the butter.
3) Once melted, add the onion and bell pepper.
4) Cook for 4 minutes.
5) Add the garlic, ginger, turmeric, cumin, garam masala, coriander, cayenne pepper and salt. Cook for 1-2 minutes.
6) Pour in the tomatoes and coconut milk. Mix well.
7) Place the chicken on top. Cover the pot and set it to poultry.
8) Release the pressure naturally.
9) Take the chicken out of the pot and shred with forks.
10) Transfer the sauce to a blender. Blend until smooth.
11) Pour the sauce over the chicken before serving.

Serving Suggestion: Serve with fresh green salad.

Tip: An alternative would be to cook the chicken in manual setting. Cook at high pressure for 15 minutes.

Nutritional Information Per Serving:

Calories 280

Total Fat 23g

Saturated Fat 7g

Cholesterol 109mg

Sodium 862mg

Total Carbohydrates 6g

Dietary Fiber 1g

Sugars 2g

Protein 33g

Potassium 792mg

Rosemary Chicken

Serves: 4
Preparation time: 20 minutes
Ingredients:
2 chicken breasts
Salt and pepper to taste
1 cup chicken broth
2 teaspoons fresh rosemary, minced
¼ cup mayo
1 tablespoon green onions, sliced
2 tablespoons almonds, slivered
2 teaspoons lemon juice
Preparation:
1) Season the chicken with the salt and pepper.
2) Add the chicken to the Instant Pot.
3) Pour in the chicken broth.
4) Seal the pot.
5) Set it to manual.
6) Cook at high pressure for 15 minutes.
7) Release the pressure naturally.
8) Take the chicken out of the pot.
9) Shred using a fork.
10) Mix the shredded chicken with the rest of the ingredients.

Serving Suggestion: Serve on top of Romaine lettuce leaves.

Tip: You can also slice the chicken breasts in cubes.

Nutritional Information Per Serving:
Calories 249
Total Fat 15g
Saturated Fat 6g
Cholesterol 65mg
Sodium 199mg
Total Carbohydrates 1g
Protein 22g
Potassium 216mg

Chicken Carnitas

Serves: 4

Preparation time: 30 minutes

Ingredients:

2 teaspoons ground cumin

1 teaspoon dried oregano

½ teaspoon ground cinnamon

1 teaspoon chili powder

2 lb. chicken thighs

Salt and pepper to taste

¼ cup orange juice

¼ cup lime juice

4 cloves garlic, minced

1 bay leaf

6 tablespoons olive oil

Preparation:

1) Combine the oregano, cumin, cinnamon and chili powder in a bowl.
2) Season the chicken with the salt and pepper.
3) Sprinkle generously both sides of the chicken with the spice mixture.
4) Pour the orange juice and lime juice into the Instant Pot.
5) Add the chicken. Sprinkle the garlic on top. Add the bay leaf. Seal the pot.
6) Choose manual mode. Cook at high pressure for 8 minutes.
7) Release the pressure quickly.
8) Slice the chicken in cubes.
9) Press the sauté setting in the Instant Pot.
10) Pour in the olive oil.
11) Brown the chicken and serve.

Serving Suggestion: Serve with any of these options: guacamole, sour cream, fresh cilantro, shredded cabbage.

Tip: Use freshly squeezed juices for this recipe.

Nutritional Information Per Serving:

Calories 630

Total Fat 38.2g

Saturated Fat 7.7g

Cholesterol 202mg

Sodium 204mg

Total Carbohydrate 3.9g

Dietary Fiber 0.7g

Total Sugars 1.4g

Protein 66.2g

Potassium 633mg

Buffalo Chicken with Cauliflower

Serves: 6
Preparation time: 30 minutes
Ingredients:
2 cups chicken, cooked and sliced into cubes
1 head cauliflower, chopped
¼ cup ranch dressing
½ cup buffalo sauce
Salt and pepper to taste
½ cup cream cheese, cubed
2 cups cheddar cheese, shredded
Preparation:
1) Add the chicken, cauliflower, ranch dressing, buffalo sauce, salt and pepper in the Instant Pot.
2) Mix well.
3) Cover the pot.
4) Choose manual mode.
5) Cook at high pressure for 5 minutes.
6) Release the pressure quickly.
7) Stir in the cream cheese and top with the cheddar before serving.

Serving Suggestion: Garnish with chopped parsley or dried basil.

Tip: You can also cook the chicken in the Instant Pot by using the sauté function.

Nutritional Information Per Serving:
Calories 344
Total fat 24.8g
Saturated Fat 12.4g
Cholesterol 100mg
Sodium 778.8mg
Carbohydrates 7.7g
Fiber 2.3g
Total Sugars 3g
Protein 23.8g
Potassium 290.3mg

Chapter 12: Keto Diet Fish & Seafood Recipes

Shrimp Scampi

Serves: 2
Preparation time: 5 minutes
Cooking Time: 2 hours 30 minutes
Ingredients:
1/2 lb raw shrimp, peeled and deveined
1/8 cup chicken broth
1 tbsp butter
1/2 tbsp lemon juice
1/4 cup white cooking wine
Directions:
Combine everything in the crock-pot. Add salt and pepper (and red pepper flakes if desired) to taste.
Cover and cook for 2.5 hours on low.
Nutritional Value:
Calories: 256, Fat: 14.7g, Net Carbs: 2g, Protein: 23.3g, Sodium: 466mg
Serving suggestions: Serve with grated parmesan and parsley on top if desired

Poached Salmon in Court-Bouillon Recipe

Serves: 2
Preparation time: 5 minutes
Cooking Time: 2 hours 30 minutes
Ingredients:
2 whole black peppercorns
1/2 medium carrot, thinly sliced
1/2 celery rib, thinly sliced
2 salmon steaks in 1-inch-thick slices
1 1/2 tbsp white wine vinegar
Directions:
Put everything in the crock-pot except for the salmon. You can also add parsley and bay leaf for extra flavor.
Rub salmon slices with salt and pepper to taste.
Cover and cook for 2 hours on high.
Spoon some of the liquid over the top. Cover and cook on high for another 30 minutes.
Nutritional Value:
Calories: 197, Fat: 7.7g, Net Carbs: 4.8g, Protein: 18.3g, Cholesterol: 95mg, Sodium: 366mg
Serving suggestions: This recipe can be enjoyed either hot or chilled.
Tip: To test if the fish is done, make a slight cut on the fish. It should be semi-transparent.

Braised Squid with Tomatoes and Fennel

Serves: 2
Preparation time: 20 minutes
Cooking Time: 4 hours
Ingredients:
1 1/2 cups clam juice
1 can plum tomatoes
1/2 fennel bulb, minced
3 tbsp all-purpose flour
1 lb squid in 1-inch pieces
Directions:
Add chopped onions, fennel and garlic to the flameproof insert of a crockpot and cook on a stove in medium heat for about 5 minutes.
Whisk in flour and tomato paste until fully mixed. Add the clam juice, tomatoes, 1 tsp salt and pepper. Boil for about 2 minutes.
Transfer to the crock-pot, cover and cook for 3 hours on low.
Uncover, add the squid and mix well. Cook for another 1 hour.
Nutritional Value:
Calories: 210, Fat: 25g, Net Carbs: 6g, Protein: 29g
Tip: Add a little white wine after adding the flour for extra flavor.

Seafood Stir-Fry Soup

Serves: 2
Preparation time: 30 minutes
Cooking Time: 3 hours
Ingredients:
7.25 oz low-carb udon noodle, beef flavor
1/2 lb shrimp
1/4 lb scallops
3 cups low-sodium broth
1 carrot, shredded
Directions:
Add all ingredients except noodles, shrimp and scallops to the crock-pot. Include seasonings such as garlic, ginger, salt and pepper to taste. Add vinegar, soy sauce and fish sauce, 1/2 tbsp each. Stir to mix well.
Cook on high for 2-3 hours.
Add udon noodles, shrimp and scallops. Cook on high for additional 10-15 minutes.
Nutritional Value:
Calories: 266, Fat: 19g, Net Carbs: 8g, Protein: 27.5g, Cholesterol: 173mg, Sodium: 489mg
Tip: Optional garnish can be sprouts, red chili flakes, jalapeno or other extra spices.

Shrimp Fajita Soup

Serves: 2
Preparation time: 20 minutes
Cooking Time: 2 hours
Ingredients:

1/2 lb shrimp
32 oz chicken broth
1 tbsp fajita seasoning
1/2 bell pepper, sliced or diced

Directions:
Put all the ingredients except the shrimp to crock-pot.
Add onion slices to taste and stir to mix well.
Cook on high for 2 hours.
Add the shrimp and cook for additional 5-15 minutes.

Nutritional Value:
Calories: 165, Fat: 7.3g, Net Carbs: 3.7g, Protein: 15.9g, Cholesterol: 87mg, Sodium: 215mg
Serving suggestions: Mushrooms, zucchini, corn, even black beans all make great additions to the recipe.

Fish and Tomatoes

Serves: 2
Preparation time: 7 minutes
Cooking Time: 3 hours
Ingredients:

1/2 bell pepper, sliced
1/8 cup low-sodium broth
8 oz diced tomatoes
1/2 tbsp rosemary
1/2 lb cod

Directions:
Put all the ingredients except the fish in the crock-pot. Add garlic, salt and pepper to taste.
Season fish with your favorite seasoning and place other ingredient in the pot.
Cook for 3 hours on low.

Nutritional Value:
Calories: 204, Fat: 16.8g, Net Carbs: 5g, Protein: 25.3g, Cholesterol: 75mg, Sodium: 296mg
Serving suggestions: Season with red pepper flakes for extra spice.

Salmon in Creamy Herb Sauce

Serves: 4
Preparation time: 20 minutes
Ingredients:

1 teaspoon garlic, minced
4 salmon fillets
½ cup heavy cream
1 teaspoon lemon juice
1 cup parmesan cheese, grated

1 tablespoon fresh dill
1 tablespoon fresh chives, chopped
1 tablespoon fresh parsley, chopped
Salt and pepper to taste

Preparation:

1) Pour ½ cup of water into the Instant Pot.
2) Add the garlic.
3) Place the steamer rack inside the pot.
4) Put the salmon on the rack.
5) Cover the pot.
6) Set it to manual.
7) Cook at high pressure for 5 minutes.
8) Release the pressure quickly.
9) Transfer the salmon to a plate.
10) Remove the steamer rack.
11) Press the sauté setting.
12) Stir in the heavy cream.
13) Simmer for 3 minutes.
14) Add the rest of the ingredients before serving.

Serving Suggestion: Serve with buttered vegetables.
Tip: Make sure that you use freshly squeezed lemon juice.
Nutritional Information Per Serving:

Calories 314
Total Fat 18.1g
Saturated Fat 6g
Cholesterol 104mg
Sodium 152mg
Total Carbohydrate 1.5g
Dietary Fiber 0.2g
Total Sugars 0.1g
Protein 37.4g

Potassium 733mg

Salmon & Spinach Pesto

Serves: 4
Preparation time: 30 minutes
Ingredients:

2 cloves garlic

¼ cup walnuts

10 cups baby spinach

1 cup parmesan, grated

½ cup olive oil

Salt and pepper to taste

1 tablespoon butter

16 oz. low carb pasta

12 oz. smoked salmon, sliced

1 ½ cup heavy cream, divided

1 teaspoon lemon zest, grated

1 teaspoon lemon juice

Preparation:

1) Add the garlic, walnuts, spinach, parmesan, olive oil, salt and pepper in a food processor.
2) Pulse until pureed.
3) Choose the manual setting in the Instant Pot.
4) Pour in 4 cups of water.
5) Add the butter and pasta.
6) Cover the pot.
7) Choose manual setting.
8) Cook at high pressure for 4 minutes.
9) Release the pressure quickly.
10) Select the sauté setting.
11) Add the rest of the ingredients.
12) Mix well.
13) Simmer for 1-2 minutes.

Serving Suggestion: Sprinkle with more parmesan cheese on top before serving.

Tip: Use basil in place of spinach if you prefer the traditional pesto flavor.

Nutritional Information Per Serving:

Calories 667

Total Fat 58.8g

Saturated Fat 18.4g

Cholesterol 94mg

Sodium 934mg

Total Carbohydrate 8.7g

Dietary Fiber 3.3g

Total Sugars 2.5g

Protein 24.9g

Potassium 652mg

Asian Tuna

Serves: 2
Preparation time: 15 minutes
Ingredients:

1 tablespoon coconut oil

1 tablespoon brown sugar

2 tablespoon maple syrup

1 teaspoon paprika

3 tablespoon coconut aminos

¼ teaspoon ginger, grated

2 tuna fillets

Salt and pepper to taste

Preparation:

1) Select the sauté setting in the Instant Pot.
2) Add the coconut oil and brown sugar.
3) Cook until the sugar has been dissolved.
4) Pour in the maple syrup, paprika, coconut aminos and ginger.
5) Mix well.
6) Place the tuna fillets on top.
7) Season with the salt and pepper.
8) Cover the pot.
9) Set it to manual.
10) Cook at low pressure for 2 minutes.
11) Release the pressure naturally.

Serving Suggestion: Sprinkle sesame seeds and chopped fresh scallions on top before serving.

Tip: You can also use other types of fish for this recipe.

Nutritional Information Per Serving:

Calories 150

Total Fat 17.8g

Saturated Fat 6.1g

Cholesterol 3mg

Sodium 8mg

Total Carbohydrate 8.5g

Dietary Fiber 0.4g

Total Sugars 16.4g

Protein 2.8g

Potassium 105mg

Fish Croquettes

Serves: 2
Preparation time: 20 minutes
Ingredients:

2 salmon fillets

Salt and pepper to taste

1 egg, beaten

¼ cup onion, chopped

2 stalks green onion, sliced

1 cup panko breadcrumbs

2 tablespoons olive oil

Preparation:

1) Pour 1 cup of water into the Instant Pot.
2) Place a steamer rack inside.
3) Add the salmon fillets on top.
4) Season both sides with the salt and pepper.
5) Cover the pot.
6) Set it to manual.
7) Cook at high pressure for 3 minutes.
8) Release the pressure quickly.
9) Take the fish out.
10) Shred the fish and add the egg, onion and green onion.
11) Add the breadcrumbs.
12) Form into patties.
13) Remove the rack and water from the pot.
14) Pour in the olive oil.
15) Add the fish patties.
16) Cook until golden.

Serving Suggestion: Serve with tartar sauce.

Tip: You can also use tuna or halibut.

Nutritional Information Per Serving:

Calories 433

Total Fat 27.5g

Saturated Fat 4.3g

Cholesterol 160mg

Sodium 181mg

Total Carbohydrate 10.1g

Dietary Fiber 1.7g

Total Sugars 1.4g

Protein 38.7g

Potassium 776mg

Shrimp & Vegetable Risotto

Serves: 4
Preparation time: 30 minutes
Ingredients:

2 teaspoons olive oil
1 bunch asparagus, sliced
3 garlic cloves, minced
½ onion, chopped
1 tablespoon butter
½ cup dry white wine
3 ½ cups chicken broth

½ cup parmesan cheese, shredded
Salt and pepper to taste
1 lb. shrimp, peeled and deveined
1 cup fresh spinach
1 tablespoon parsley, chopped
4 cups cauliflower rice
1 tablespoon lemon juice

Preparation:

1) Set the Instant Pot to sauté. Pour in half of the olive oil.
2) Cook the asparagus for 3 minutes.
3) Add the garlic and onion. Cook for 1 minute.
4) Add the butter and stir well.
5) Deglaze the pot by pouring in the white wine.
6) Add the chicken broth and parmesan. Stir well.
7) Season with the salt and pepper.   Cover the pot.
8) Set tit to manual.
9) Cook at high pressure for 8 minutes.
10) While waiting, season the shrimp with salt and pepper.
11) Release the pressure quickly.
12) Stir in the shrimp and vegetables.
13) Press sauté function. Cook for 4 minutes.
14) Stir in the cauliflower rice and drizzle with the lemon juice before serving.

Serving Suggestion: Garnish with chopped parsley.

Tip: You can also add other seafood such as squid or fish flakes.

Nutritional Information Per Serving:

Calories 277
Total Fat 9.9g
Saturated Fat 4.1g
Cholesterol 251mg
Sodium 1040mg

Total Carbohydrate 6.8g
Dietary Fiber 1g
Total Sugars 1.9g
Protein 33.4g
Potassium 524mg

Shrimp Mac & Cheese

Serves: 2

Preparation time: 20 minutes

Ingredients:

1 tablespoon butter

¼ red pepper, sliced

¼ green pepper, sliced

1 ¼ cups low carb macaroni pasta

15 shrimps, peeled and deveined

1 tablespoon Cajun spice

½ cup cheddar cheese, shredded

2/3 cup coconut milk

Preparation:

1) Choose the sauté function in the Instant Pot.
2) Add the butter.
3) Cook the peppers for 1 minute.
4) Add the pasta.
5) Pour in 2 cups of water.
6) Cover the pot.
7) Set it to manual.
8) Cook at high pressure for 3 minutes.
9) Do a quick pressure release.
10) Press the sauté mode.
11) Add the shrimp.
12) Cook for 2 minutes.
13) Stir in the rest of the ingredients before serving.

Serving Suggestion: Garnish with peeled shrimp and chopped parsley.

Tip: Use keto-friendly low carb macaroni pasta for this recipe.

Nutritional Information Per Serving:

Calories 459

Total Fat 22.2g

Saturated Fat 11.8g

Cholesterol 399mg

Sodium 902mg

Total Carbohydrate 7.1g

Dietary Fiber 1.1g

Total Sugars 6.2g

Protein 48.9g

Potassium 410mg

Chapter 13: Keto Diet Vegan & Vegetarian Recipes

Cabbage in Cream Sauce

Serves: 4-6
Preparation time: 20 minutes
Ingredients:

1 tablespoon olive oil
1 onion, chopped
1 cup bacon, diced
2 cups bone broth
4 cups cabbage, chopped

1 bay leaf
¼ teaspoon nutmeg
1 cup coconut milk
Salt to taste

Preparation:

1) Choose the sauté function in the Instant Pot. Pour in the olive oil.
2) Add the onion and cook until soft. Add the bacon and cook until golden crisp.
3) Pour in the bone broth. Scrape the bottom of the pot using a wooden spoon.
4) Add the cabbage and bay leaf. Cover the pot.
5) Press the manual mode. Cook at high pressure for 4 minutes.
6) Release the pressure naturally.
7) Press the sauté function.
8) Stir in the coconut milk.
9) Season with the salt and nutmeg.
10) Simmer for 5 minutes.

Serving Suggestion: Sprinkle parsley flakes on top.

Tip: You can also add other vegetables like young corn or spinach if you like.

Nutritional Information Per Serving:

Calories 699
Total Fat 84.3g
Saturated Fat 35.1g
Cholesterol 175mg
Sodium 380mg
Total Carbohydrate 12.4g
Dietary Fiber 3.8g
Total Sugars 5.5g
Protein 71.4g
Potassium 1360mg

Spinach & Mushroom Curry

Serves: 4
Preparation time: 20 minutes
Ingredients:

2 tablespoons olive oil
3 cloves garlic, minced
1 teaspoon cumin seeds
1 onion, chopped
1 jalapeño, sliced into quarter
3 tomatoes, chopped
1 tablespoon coriander powder

1 teaspoon garam masala
¼ teaspoon red chili powder
1 teaspoon turmeric powder
9 oz. spinach, chopped
8 oz. mushrooms, sliced
Salt to taste

Preparation:

1) Select the sauté mode in the Instant Pot.
2) Pour in the olive oil.
3) Add the garlic and cumin seeds.
4) Cook for 1 minute.
5) Add the onion and jalapeno.
6) Cook for 3 minutes.
7) Add the tomatoes and spice powders.
8) Add the rest of the ingredients.
9) Mix well.
10) Cover the pot.
11) Set it to manual.
12) Cook at high pressure for 3 minutes.
13) Release the pressure quickly.
14) Set it to sauté function.
15) Simmer until sauce is reduced.

Serving Suggestion: Serve with a cup of cauliflower rice.

Tip: Use curry powder if garam masala or coriander powder is not available.

Nutritional Information Per Serving:

Calories 245
Total Fat 25.7g
Saturated Fat 5.2g
Cholesterol 0mg

Sodium 205mg
Total Carbohydrate 9.5g
Dietary Fiber 3.9g
Total Sugars 5.8g

Protein 10.1g
Potassium 1664mg

Asparagus with Lemon

Serves: 2
Preparation time: 10 minutes
Cooking Time: 2 hours
Ingredients:
1 lb asparagus spears
1 tbsp lemon juice
Instructions:
Prepare the seasonings: 2 crushed cloves of garlic and salt and pepper to taste.
Put the asparagus spears on the bottom of the crockpot. Add the lemon juce and the seasonings.
Cook on low for 2 hours.
Nutritional Value:
Calories: 78, Fat: 2 g, Net carbs: 3.7 g, Protein: 9 g

Veggie-Noodle Soup

Serves: 2
Preparation time: 10 minutes
Cooking Time: 8 hours
Ingredients:
1/2 cup chopped carrots, chopped
1/2 cup chopped celery, chopped
1 tsp Italian seasoning
7 oz zucchini, cut spiral
2 cups spinach leaves, chopped
Instructions:
Except for the zucchini and spinach, add all the ingredients to the crockpot.
Add 3 cups of water.
Add 1/2 cup of chopped onion an garlic, 1/8 tsp of salt and pepper and desired spices such as thyme and bay leaves if desired.
Cover and cook for 8 hours on low.
Add the zucchini and spinach at the last 10 minutes of cooking.
Nutritional Value:
Calories: 56, Fat: 0.5 g, Net carbs: 0.5 g, Protein: 3 g

Tip: Use vegetable broth instead of water for extra flavor.

Zucchini and Yellow Squash

Serves: 2
Preparation time: 10 minutes
Cooking Time: 6 hours
Ingredients:
2/3 cup zucchini, sliced
2/3 cups yellow squash, sliced
1/3 tsp Italian seasoning
1/8 cup butter
Instructions:
Place zucchini and squash on the bottom of the crockpot.
Sprinkle with the Italian seasoning with salt, pepper and garlic powder to taste. Top with butter.
Cover and cook for 6 hours on low.
Nutritional Value:
Calories: 122, Fat: 9.9 g, Net carbs: 3.7 g, Protein: 4.2 g
Serving suggestions: Top with Parmesan cheese for extra flavor.

Gluten-Free Zucchini Bread

Serves: 2
Preparation time: 10 minutes
Cooking Time: 3 hours
Ingredients:
1/2 cup coconut flour
1/2 tsp baking powder and baking soda
1 egg, whisked

1/4 cup butter
1 cup zucchini, shredded

Instructions:
Combine all dry ingredients and add a pinch of salt and sweetener of choice.
Combine the dry ingredients with the eggs and mix thoroughly.
Fold in zucchini and spread at the bottom of the crockpot.
Cover and cook for 3 hours on high.
Nutritional Value:
Calories: 174, Fat: 13 g, Net carbs: 2.9 g, Protein: 4 g
Serving suggestions: This recipe is best enjoyed refrigerated.
Tip: Add 1 tsp each of cinnamon and vanilla for more flavor.

Chapter 14: Keto Diet Side Dishes & Desserts

Creamy Broccoli Mash

Serves: 4
Preparation time: 10 minutes
Ingredients:
1 tablespoon butter
3 cloves garlic, crushed
1 lb. broccoli, chopped
4 oz. cream cheese
½ cup water
Salt and pepper to taste
Preparation:
1) Set the Instant Pot to sauté.
2) Add the butter.
3) Cook the garlic for 30 seconds.
4) Add the rest of the ingredients.
5) Cover the pot.
6) Choose manual mode.
7) Cook at high pressure for 1 minute.
8) Release a pressure quickly.
9) Mash the broccoli.

Serving Suggestion: Sprinkle top with chopped chives.

Tip: Add ¼ teaspoon red pepper flakes if you want the broccoli mash a little spicy.

Nutritional Information Per Serving:
Calories 166
Total Fat 16.2g
Saturated Fat 8.1g
Cholesterol 39mg
Sodium 143mg
Total Carbohydrate 7g
Dietary Fiber 3g
Total Sugars 2g
Protein 5.5g
Potassium 403mg

Cauliflower Salad

Serves: 4

Preparation time: 15 minutes

Ingredients:

1 head cauliflower, sliced into florets

4 eggs, hard boiled

1 cup mayonnaise

1 cup bacon bits

2 tablespoons apple cider vinegar

¼ cup onion, chopped

1 teaspoon garlic, minced

¾ cup green onions, chopped

Salt and pepper to taste

Preparation:

1) Place a steamer rack inside the Instant Pot.
2) Add the cauliflower florets on top of the rack.
3) Pour in 1 ½ cups of water.
4) Seal the pot.
5) Set it to manual.
6) Cook at high pressure for 3 minutes.
7) Release the pressure quickly.
8) Remove the cauliflower from the pot.
9) Mash the cauliflower and eggs.
10) Stir in the rest of the ingredients.

Serving Suggestion: Set aside 1 hard-boiled egg, slice into wedges and use these to garnish the salad.

Tip: Use a potato masher to mash the cauliflower.

Nutritional Information Per Serving:

Calories 474

Total Fat 36g

Saturated Fat 8.2g

Cholesterol 210mg

Sodium 1161mg

Total Carbohydrate 10.7g

Dietary Fiber 2.3g

Total Sugars 6.5g

Protein 18.4g

Potassium 497mg

Deviled Egg Salad

Serves: 4

Preparation time: 25 minutes

Ingredients:

1 tablespoon olive oil

10 eggs

5 strips bacon

2 tablespoons mayonnaise

1 teaspoon Dijon mustard

¼ teaspoon smoked paprika

Preparation:

1) Grease a small cake pan with the olive oil.
2) Crack the eggs into the pan.
3) Pour 1 cup of water into the Instant Pot.
4) Place a steamer rack inside the pot.
5) Put the cake pan on top of the rack.
6) Cover the pot.
7) Choose manual setting.
8) Cook at high pressure for 6 minutes.
9) Release the pressure naturally.
10) Flip the pan onto a chopping board.
11) Chop up the egg.
12) Remove the rack and water from the pot.
13) Set it to sauté.
14) Cook the bacon until golden crisp.
15) Transfer the bacon to a chopping board and chop.
16) Mix the eggs, bacon and the rest of the ingredients.

Serving Suggestion: Garnish with chopped green onion.

Tip: Chill in the refrigerator before serving.

Nutritional Information Per Serving:

Calories 346

Total Fat 26.9g

Saturated Fat 7.5g

Cholesterol 437mg

Sodium 769mg

Total Carbohydrate 3.1g

Dietary Fiber 0.1g

Total Sugars 1.3g

Protein 22.8g

Potassium 287mg

Balsamic Mushrooms

Serves: 4

Preparation time: 15 minutes

Ingredients:

¼ cup olive oil

3 cloves garlic, minced

1 lb. fresh mushrooms, sliced

3 tablespoons balsamic vinegar

Salt and pepper to taste

Preparation:

1) Press the sauté button in the Instant Pot.
2) Add the olive oil.
3) Add the garlic cloves and mushrooms.
4) Toss to coat with oil.
5) Cook for 3 minutes.
6) Add the vinegar.
7) Cook for 2 minutes.
8) Season with the salt and pepper.

Serving Suggestion: Sprinkle top with chopped garlic chives.

Tip: You can also add 3 tablespoons white wine after adding the vinegar.

Nutritional Information Per Serving:

Calories 138

Total Fat 12.9g

Saturated Fat 1.8g

Cholesterol 0mg

Sodium 7mg

Total Carbohydrate 4.6g

Dietary Fiber 1.2g

Total Sugars 2g

Protein 3.7g

Potassium 378mg

Easy Cheesecake

Serves: 2
Preparation time: 15 minutes
Cooking Time: 2 hours 30 minutes
Ingredients:
24 oz cream cheese
3 eggs
1 cup gluten-free sweetener
½ tbsp vanilla
Instructions:
Mix all ingredients thoroughly using a mixer in a bowl.
Pour 2 to 3 cups of water in the crockpot and place the bowl inside.
Cover and cook for 2 hours and 30 minutes on high.
Nutritional Value:
Calories: 207, Fat: 16.1 g, Net carbs: 5.7 g, Protein: 7.8 g
Serving suggestions: Serve with any low-sugar fruit sauce or sliced fruits.

Blueberry Lemon Custard Cake

Serves: 2
Preparation time: 15 minutes
Cooking Time: 3 hours
Ingredients:
2 eggs
1/4 cup coconut flour
1/8 cup lemon juice
1/8 cup sweetener
1/4 cup fresh blueberries
Instructions:
Mix all ingredients, except blueberries, thoroughly using a mixer in a bowl.
Pour the mixture in the crockpot.
Cover and cook for 3 hours on high.
Nutritional Value:
Calories: 140, Fat: 9.2 g, Net carbs: 5.1 g, Protein: 3.9 g
Serving suggestions: This recipe is best served chilled with whipped cream on top.
Tip: You will know the recipe is cooked when a toothpick comes out clean when the cake is poked.

Crustless Beef Pizza

Serves: 2
Preparation time: 15 minutes
Cooking Time: 4 hours
Ingredients:

3/4 cup pizza sauce
1 lb ground beef, browned
1 cup mozzarella cheese

pizza toppings of your choice (pepperoni, mushrooms, peppers, etc.)

Instructions:

Mix the ground beef and mozzarella in the crockpot then spread evenly across the bottom.

Top it with pizza sauce then put the desired toppings.

Cover and cook for 4 hours on low.

Nutritional Value:

Calories: 178, Fat: 9.8 g, Net carbs: 4/8 g, Protein: 10.4 g

Serving suggestions: Serve with some Parmesan cheese.

Tip: You will know the recipe is cooked when a toothpick comes out clean when the cake is poked.

Choco Swirl Cheesecake

Serves: 2
Preparation time: 15 minutes
Cooking Time: 2 hours 30 minutes
Ingredients:

24 oz cream cheese
3 eggs
1 cup gluten-free sweetener

½ tbsp vanilla
3/4 cup unsweetened chocolate, melted

Instructions:

Mix all ingredients, except chocolate, thoroughly using a mixer in a bowl.

Pour the melted chocolate on the bowl and use a knife to swirl it into the batter.

Pour 2 to 3 cups of water in the crockpot and place the bowl inside.

Cover and cook for 2 hours and 30 minutes on high.

Nutritional Value:

Calories: 232, Fat: 17.3 g, Net carbs: 6.1 g, Protein: 8.1 g

Serving suggestions: Serve with any low-sugar fruit sauce or sliced fruits.

Chapter 15: Keto Diet Soups, Broth & Stews

Asparagus Soup

Serves: 6

Preparation time: 1 hour and 10 minutes

Ingredients:

3 tablespoons ghee

1 white onion, chopped

5 cloves garlic, crushed

4 cups chicken broth

1 cup ham, diced

2 lb. asparagus, sliced in half

½ teaspoon dried thyme

Salt and pepper to taste

Preparation:

1) Select the sauté function in the Instant Pot.
2) Add the ghee.
3) Add the onion and cook for 5 minutes.
4) Add the garlic, broth and ham.
5) Simmer for 3 minutes.
6) Add the asparagus and thyme.
7) Secure the pot.
8) Choose soup setting.
9) Cook for 45 minutes.
10) Blend the mixture in a food processor.
11) Season with the salt and pepper.

Serving Suggestion: Garnish with low-carb croutons.

Tip: You can also use an immersion blender instead of a food processor.

Nutritional Information Per Serving:

Calories 160

Total Fat 13.4g

Saturated Fat 7.9g

Cholesterol 29mg

Sodium 807mg

Total Carbohydrate 6.9g

Dietary Fiber 4g

Total Sugars 4.1g

Protein 10.7g

Carrot Soup

Serves: 4

Preparation time: 20 minutes

Ingredients:

½ onion, diced

1 clove garlic, minced

8 carrots, sliced into cubes

2 cups vegetable broth

15 oz. coconut milk

Salt and pepper to taste

Preparation:

1) Press the sauté button in the Instant Pot.
2) Add the oil.
3) Sauté onion and garlic for 1-3 minutes.
4) Add the carrots, vegetable broth and coconut milk.
5) Season with the salt and pepper.
6) Seal the pot.
7) Choose manual mode.
8) Cook at high pressure for 8 minutes.
9) Release the pressure naturally.
10) Use an immersion blender to blend the soup until smooth.

Serving Suggestion: Serve this soup with coconut cream and top with chopped parsley.

Tip: You can also use a regular blender to blend the soup.

Nutritional Information Per Serving:

Calories 320

Total Fat 26g

Saturated Fat 22.7g

Cholesterol 0mg

Sodium 482mg

Total Carbohydrate 19.9g

Dietary Fiber 5.7g

Total Sugars 10.5g

Protein 6.1g

Potassium 796mg

Spring Keto Stew with Venison

Serves: 2
Preparation time: 20 minutes
Cooking Time: 6 hours
Ingredients:
1 lb venison stew meat
1/2 cup purple cabbage, shredded
1/2 cup celery, sliced
2 cup bone broth
Instructions:
Sauté cabbage and celery with olive oil and garlic in a skillet.
Add the venison and season with salt and pepper to taste. Stir until meat is browned.
Transfer everything into the crockpot. Add the cone broth.
Cover and cook on low for 6 hours.
Nutritional Value:
Calories: 310, Fat: 16 g, Net carbs: 5 g, Protein: 32 g
Serving suggestions: When cooked, add the asparagus for extra flavor and greens. Serve with lime if desired.

Mexican Taco Soup

Serves: 2
Preparation time: 5 minutes
Cooking Time: 4 hours
Ingredients:
1 lb ground meat, browned
8 oz cream cheese
10 oz diced tomatoes and chilis
1 tbsp of taco seasonings
1 cup of chicken broth
Instructions:
Combine all ingredients in the crockpot.
Cook on low for 4 hours.
Nutritional Value:
Calories: 547, Fat: 43 g, Net carbs: 5 g, Protein: 33 g
Serving suggestions: Stir in cilantro or garnish with shredded cheese before serving.

Oxtail Stew

Serves: 2
Preparation time: 20 minutes
Cooking Time: 10 hours
Ingredients:
2 lb oxtail, chopped
10 tomatoes, diced
4 tsp paprika
Instructions:
Place oxtail in the crockpot with water filling up to half the pot.
Cover and cook for 10 hours on low.
When cooked, transfer the oxtail to a saucepan and add the tomatoes paprika and other desired seasonings (garlic cloves, chili powder, salt).
Stew for 15 minutes.
Nutritional Value:
Calories: 456, Fat: 29 g, Net carbs: 7 g, Protein: 37 g

Rabbit Stew

Serves: 2
Preparation time: 20 minutes
Cooking Time: 6 hours
Ingredients:
1 rabbit, browned
1 lb andouille sausage, cut to 1/2 inches thick
3 medium carrots, 1-inch chunks
2 qt chicken stock
Spices of choice
Instructions:
Sauté onion, sausage and desired spices in a skillet, then add half of the stock to deglaze.
Put the rabbit in the crockpot and add the contents of the skillet.
Cover and cook for 6 hours on high.
Nutritional Value:
Calories: 381, Fat: 32 g, Net carbs: 4 g, Protein: 29 g
Tip: You can add mushrooms for extra flavor.

Chapter 16: Keto Diet Weekend & Festival Recipes

Chicken Fajitas

Serves: 8
Preparation time: 20 minutes
Ingredients:

4 chicken breasts
Salt and pepper to taste
1 tablespoon fajita seasoning
1 onion, sliced into quarters
2 cloves garlic

1 ½ cup chicken broth
1 teaspoon olive oil
8 low carb tortillas
2 red bell peppers, sliced into strips and grilled

Preparation:

1) Season the chicken breasts with salt, pepper and fajita seasoning.
2) Place inside the Instant Pot.
3) Add the onion and garlic on top of the chicken.
4) Pour in the chicken broth.
5) Lock the lid in place.
6) Set it to manual.
7) Cook at high pressure for 5 minutes.
8) Release the pressure naturally.
9) Let the chicken cool and then shred using a fork.
10) Top the tortillas with shredded chicken and grilled bell peppers and wrap.

Serving Suggestion: You can also add other toppings such as salsa, sour cream, Romaine lettuce, and cilantro.
Tip: You can also sauté the bell pepper in the Instant Pot if you don't have time to grill.
Nutritional Information Per Serving:

Calories 338
Total Fat 12.3g
Saturated Fat 3g
Cholesterol 125mg
Sodium 441mg
Total Carbohydrate 6.8g
Dietary Fiber 4.2g
Total Sugars 2.2g
Protein 43.4g

Potassium 458mg

Beef Nachos

Serves: 6
Preparation time: 20 minutes
Ingredients:
1 tablespoon olive oil
2 ½ cups ground beef
1 tablespoon taco seasoning
12 oz. low carb tortilla chips
2 cups cheddar cheese, shredded
3 tablespoons sour cream
Preparation:
1) Set the Instant Pot to sauté.
2) Add the olive oil.
3) Add the ground beef.
4) Season with the taco seasoning.
5) Cook until brown.
6) Arrange the tortilla chips on a baking pan.
7) Spread sour cream on top.
8) Sprinkle cooked beef and cheese.
9) Bake in the oven until the cheese has melted.

Serving Suggestion: Serve with fresh cilantro and salsa.

Tip: You can also use other types of cheese depending on your preference.
Nutritional Information Per Serving:
Calories 778
Total Fat 47g
Saturated Fat 7g
Cholesterol 32mg
Sodium 477mg
Total Carbohydrates 8g
Dietary Fiber 3g
Sugars 1g
Protein 33g
Potassium 158mg

Barbecue Sliders

Serves: 12
Preparation time: 15 minutes
Ingredients:
4 cups pork strips
1 cup water
2 cups keto-friendly barbecue sauce
12 keto slider buns
Preparation:
1) Season the pork strips with salt and pepper.
2) Place inside the Instant Pot.
3) Pour in the water.
4) Secure the pot.
5) Press the manual button.
6) Cook at high pressure for 10 minutes.
7) Release the pressure naturally.
8) Discard the water.
9) Press the sauté setting.
10) Add the barbecue sauce and simmer for 5 minutes.
11) Put the pork strips inside the Instant Pot.
12) Stuff the slider buns with barbecue meat.

Serving Suggestion: Add Romaine lettuce or avocado cubes to the slider.
Tip: Keto slider buns are made with almond flour.
Nutritional Information Per Serving:
Calories 427
Total Fat 14.5g
Saturated Fat 3g
Cholesterol 24mg
Sodium 1244mg
Total Carbohydrate 31.4g
Dietary Fiber 0.3g
Total Sugars 10.9g
Protein 2.9g
Potassium 132mg

Bacon Wrapped Stuffed Chicken Rolls

Serves: 2

Preparation time: 45 minutes

Ingredients:

2 chicken breasts fillets

1 ham, sliced in half

6 asparagus spears, trimmed

8 strips bacon

4 slices Mozzarella cheese

Salt and pepper to taste

Preparation:

1) Flatten the chicken breast using a rolling pin or meat mallet.
2) Season both sides of the chicken fillets with salt and pepper.
3) Place cheese slices, cooked ham and asparagus spears on top of the chicken fillets.
4) Roll each of the fillets tightly.
5) Wrap each chicken roll with bacon slices.
6) Secure with toothpicks.
7) Add 1 cup of water into the Instant Pot.
8) Place a steamer rack inside.
9) Put the chicken rolls on top of the rack.
10) Cover the pot.
11) Choose manual setting.
12) Cook at high pressure for 7 minutes.
13) Release the pressure naturally.
14) Discard the water and remove the rack.
15) Press the sauté setting in the Instant Pot.
16) Cook the rolls until the bacon has turned golden crispy.

Serving Suggestion: Serve with leafy green salad.

Tip: Let cool a little before slicing.

Nutritional Information Per Serving:

Calories 586

Total Fat 41.8g

Saturated Fat 16.5g

Cholesterol 114mg

Sodium 2097mg

Total Carbohydrate 5.9g

Dietary Fiber 1.5g

Total Sugars 1.4g

Protein 45.7g

Potassium 575mg

Conclusion

There are many good reasons the ketogenic diet is widely used today in many parts of the world.

As science has proven (and users can attest), it is a highly effective means of losing weight safely. It helps the body burn more fat using the process of ketosis, which was explained in detail in this book.

But that's not all. The keto diet has also been shown to have various benefits for the health—lowering blood pressure and cholesterol levels, reducing the risk of many ailments, improving mental health and many more.

When you make use of this diet, you will not only be able to finally achieve the weight and figure you desire, you can also keep yourself in top health and ward off chronic ailments.

Of course, the diet program is not without drawbacks, risks and side effects. All these were also discussed in this book. The good news is, there are solutions to all of these. The simple solutions and strategies will help you breeze through the adjustment period a lot more easily.

Hopefully, with all the information about the ketogenic diet provided in this book, along with the 80+ delicious and simple keto-friendly recipes, we are able to help you get started with this meaningful journey.
Good luck!

Appendix I: Measurement Conversion Chart

Unit	Conversion	Conversion
1 teaspoon	1/3 tablespoon	1/6 ounce
1 tablespoon	3 teaspoons	½ ounce
1/8 cup	2 tablespoons	1 ounce
¼ cup	4 tablespoons	2 ounces
1/3 cup	¼ cup and 4 teaspoons	2 ¾ ounces
½ cup	8 tablespoons	4 ounces
1 cup	½ pint	8 ounces
1 pint	2 cups	16 ounces
1 quart	4 cups	32 ounces
1 liter	1 quart and ¼ cup	4 ¼ cups
1 gallon	4 quarts	16 cups

Appendix II: Keto Living Websites

Ketogenic.com (https://ketogenic.com/)

Ruled Me (https://www.ruled.me/)

Ketogasm (https://ketogasm.com/)

Diet Doctor (https://www.dietdoctor.com/low-carb/keto)

Keto Connect (https://www.ketoconnect.net/)

The Keto - Weekly Digest for the Keto Community (https://sites.google.com/view/theketo)

Living' La Vida Low-Carb (http://livinlavidalowcarb.com/)

The Ketogenic Diet Resource (http://www.ketogenic-diet-resource.com/)

A Guide to Ketosis (http://josepharcita.blogspot.co.uk/2011/03/guide-to-ketosis.html)

Caveman Keto (http://cavemanketo.com/)

Diet Doctor - LCHF for Beginners (http://www.dietdoctor.com/lchf)

Healthy Keto (http://healthyketo.com/)

Mona Leigh Sims - Food & Health (http://www.monasims.com/foodie1.htm)

Peter Attia's Eating Academy (http://eatingacademy.com/)

The Keto Diet (http://www.reddit.com/r/theketodiet/)

85925821R00060

Made in the USA
San Bernardino, CA
24 August 2018